VISITORS' ATLAS & GUIDE

A-Z DEVON CORNWALL WEST SOMERSET

CW00409839

CONTENTS

St Michaels Mount

Geographers' A-Z Map Company Ltd

Fairfield Road, Borough Green,
Sevenoaks, Kent TN15 8PP

Enquiries & Trade Sales
01732 781000

Retail Sales
01732 783422

www.a-zmaps.co.uk

Every possible care has been taken to ensure that, to the best of our knowledge, the information contained in this atlas is accurate at the date of publication. However, we cannot warrant that our work is entirely error free and whilst we would be grateful to learn of any inaccuracies, we do not accept any responsibility for loss or damage resulting from reliance on information contained within this publication.

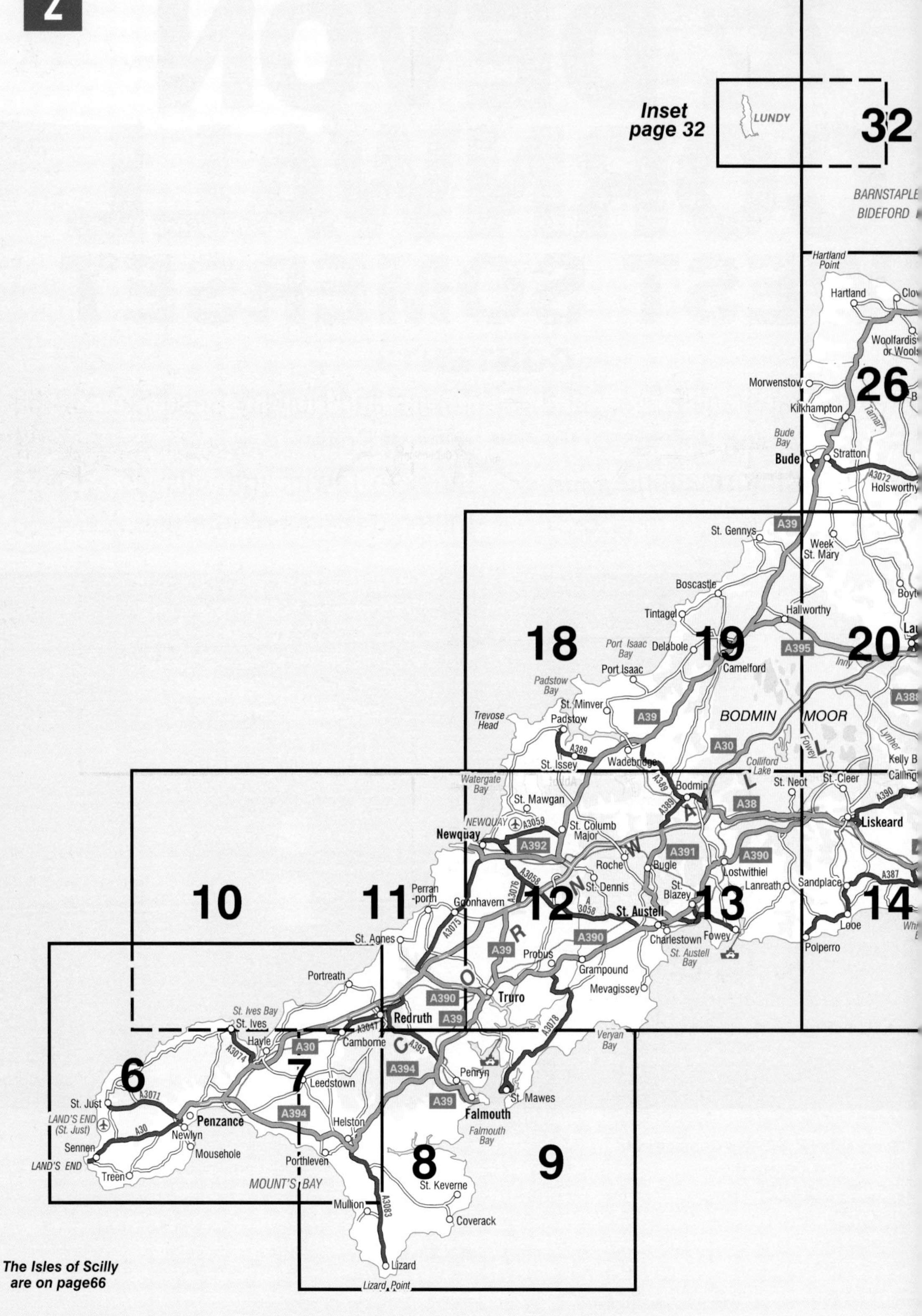

The Isles of Scilly are on page66

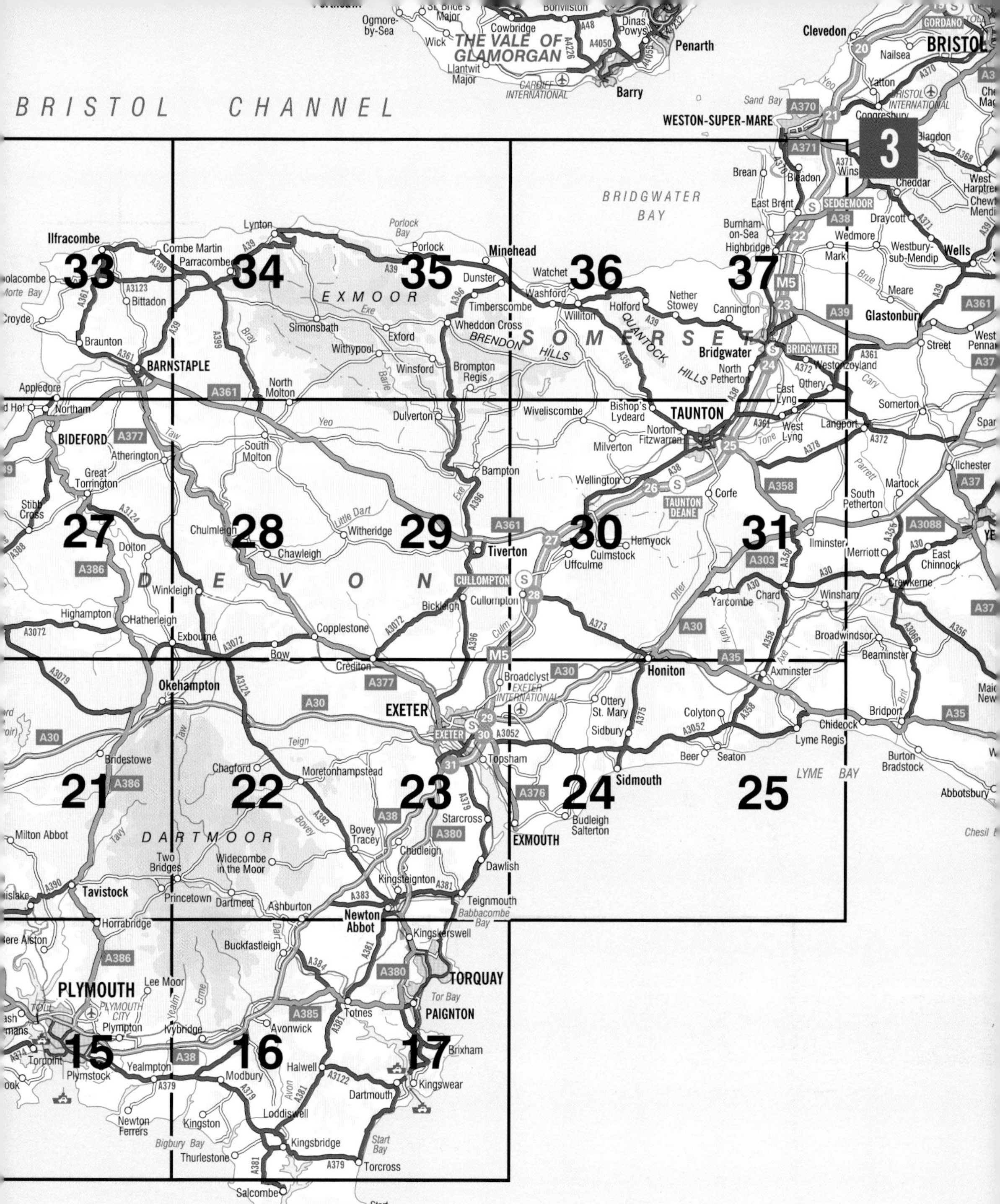

3

BRISTOL CHANNEL

Ogmore-by-Sea
St Bride's Major
Bonvilston
Cowbridge
Wick
THE VALE OF GLAMORGAN
Llantwit Major
CARDIFF INTERNATIONAL
Dinas Powys
Penarth
Barry
Clevedon
GORDANO
BRISTOL
Nailsea
Yatton
BRISTOL INTERNATIONAL
Congresbury
Sand Bay
WESTON-SUPER-MARE
Blagdon
Winscombe
Cheddar
West Harptree
Brean
Bleadon
East Brent
SEDGEMOOR
BRIDGWATER BAY
Burnham-on-Sea
Highbridge
Draycott
Wedmore
Mark
Westbury-sub-Mendip
Wells
Meare
Glastonbury
Street
Porlock Bay
Porlock
Minehead
Lynton
Ilfracombe
Combe Martin
Parracombe
Mortehoe
Morte Bay
Croyde
Bittadon
Braunton
BARNSTAPLE
EXMOOR
Simonsbath
Exford
Withypool
Winsford
Dunster
Timberscombe
Wheddon Cross
BRENDON HILLS
Brompton Regis
Watchet
Washford
Williton
Holford
Nether Stowey
Cannington
QUANTOCK HILLS
SOMERSET
Bridgwater
BRIDGWATER
North Petherton
Westonzoyland
East Lyng
Othery
Appledore
Northam
BIDEFORD
North Molton
South Molton
Atherington
Great Torrington
Dulverton
Wiveliscombe
Bishop's Lydeard
TAUNTON
Norton Fitzwarren
Milverton
West Lyng
Langport
Somerton
Bampton
Wellington
TAUNTON DEANE
Corfe
South Petherton
Martock
Ilchester
Stibb Cross
Dolton
Chulmleigh
Chawleigh
Witheridge
Tiverton
Hemyock
Culmstock
Uffculme
Ilminster
Merriott
East Chinnock
Crewkerne
DEVON
CULLOMPTON
Cullompton
Winkleigh
Highampton
Hatherleigh
Exbourne
Bow
Copplestone
Crediton
Bickleigh
Chard
Yarcombe
Winsham
Broadwindsor
Beaminster
Honiton
Axminster
Okehampton
Broadclyst
EXETER INTERNATIONAL
EXETER
Ottery St. Mary
Sidbury
Colyton
Chideock
Bridport
Lyme Regis
Bridestowe
Chagford
Moretonhampstead
Topsham
Beer
Seaton
Burton Bradstock
LYME BAY
Sidmouth
Budleigh Salterton
EXMOUTH
Abbotsbury
Chesil Beach
Milton Abbot
DARTMOOR
Bovey Tracey
Starcross
Chudleigh
Two Bridges
Widecombe in the Moor
Dawlish
Tavistock
Princetown
Dartmeet
Ashburton
Kingsteignton
Teignmouth
Babbacombe Bay
Horrabridge
Newton Abbot
Bere Alston
Buckfastleigh
Kingskerswell
TORQUAY
PLYMOUTH
Lee Moor
PLYMOUTH CITY
Tor Bay
Totnes
PAIGNTON
Plympton
Ivybridge
Avonwick
Brixham
Torpoint
Plymstock
Yealmpton
Modbury
Halwell
Kingswear
Dartmouth
Newton Ferrers
Kingston
Loddiswell
Bigbury Bay
Thurlestone
Kingsbridge
Start Bay
Torcross
Salcombe
Start Point

33 34 35 36 37
27 28 29 30 31
21 22 23 24 25
15 16 17

REFERENCE

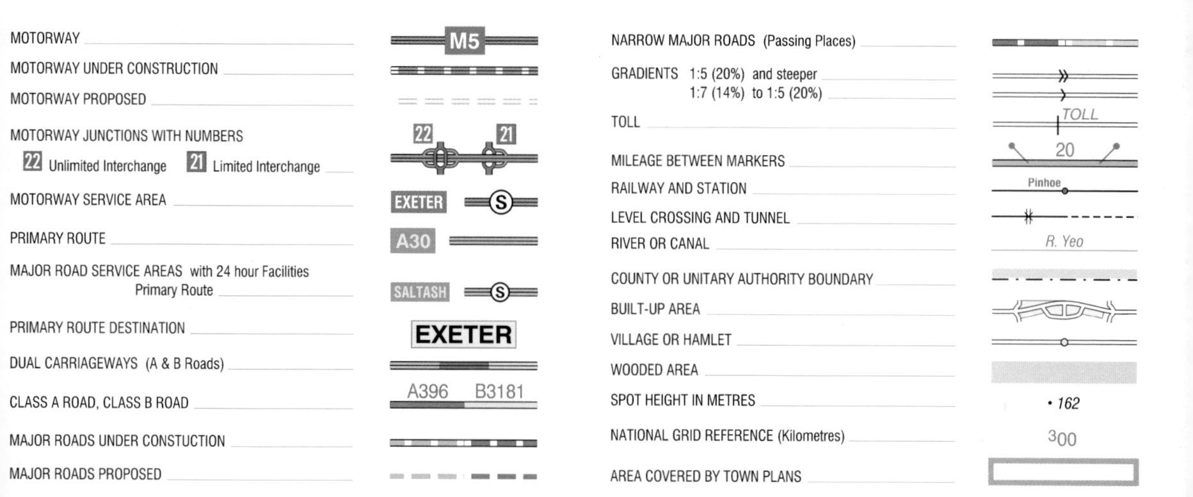

TOURIST INFORMATION

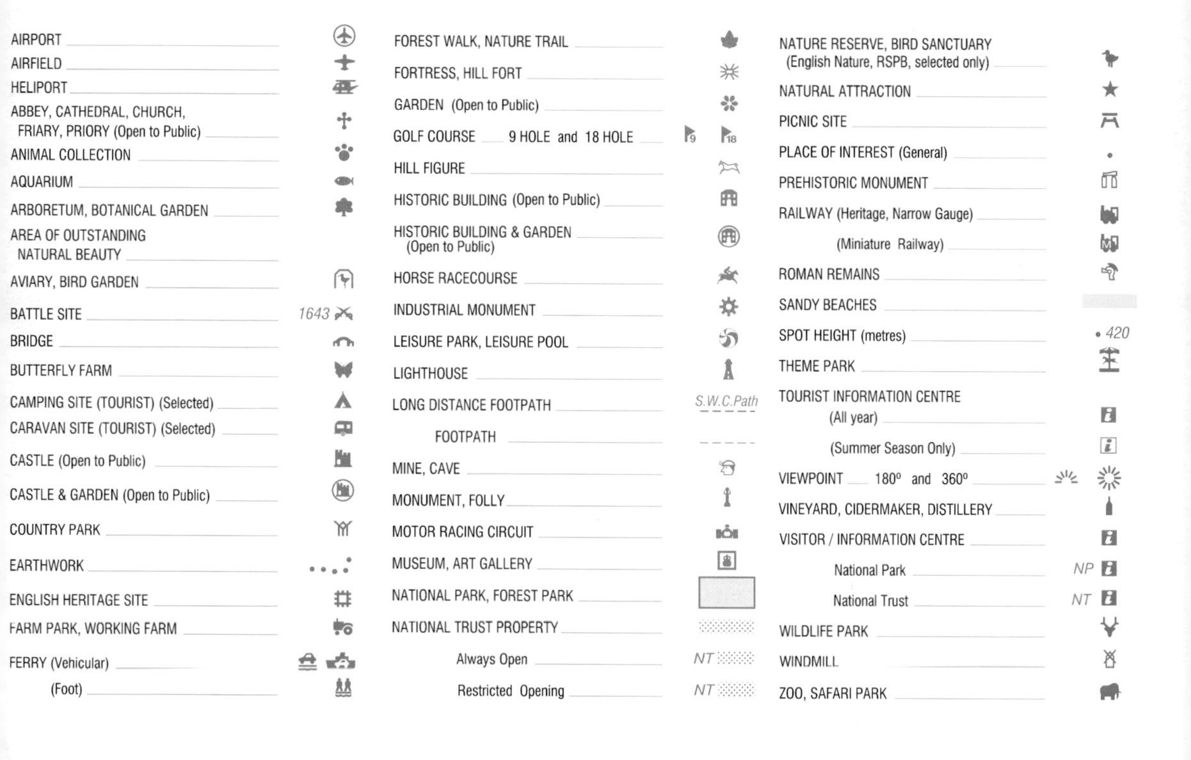

1: 158,400

SCALE

2.5 Miles to 1 inch
1.584 Kms (0.98 Miles) to 1 cm

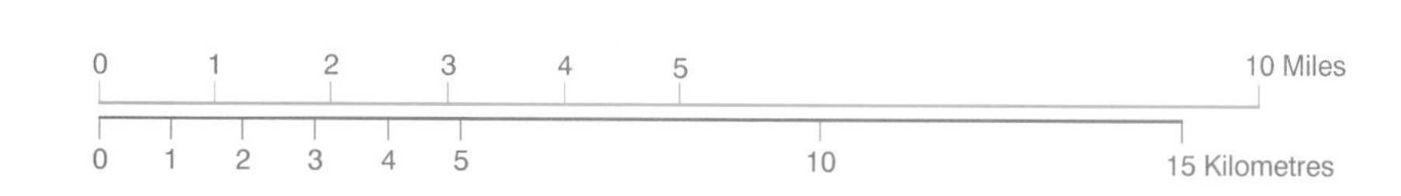

LAND'S END PENINSULA

The south-west peninsula of Cornwall, known by the Cornish name Penwith, is a flat granite mass with dramatic cliff scenery. Land's End is the most westerly point of mainland England - 1 mile directly to the west can be seen Longships Lighthouse (built 1873), whilst Wolf Rock Lighthouse is 9 miles south-west and 19 miles further are the Isles of Scilly, just visible on a clear day. Land's End is home to a variety of attractions including Return to the Last Labyrinth, Air Sea Rescue, The Relentless Sea, The First and Last Inn and the obligatory Land's End Signpost. Sennen is the most western village situated near the popular long sandy beach of Whitesand Bay, frequented by surfers. Inland, (Chapel) Carn Brea is owned by the National Trust and at 200 m (657 ft) is the first and last hill in England, reputed to have the widest sea view visible from the mainland in the British Isles.

At Porthcurno is The Minack Open-Air Theatre (with the adjoining Rowena Cade Exhibition Centre), a cliff edge amphitheatre in classical Greek style utilizing the sea and sky as a backcloth. Also here is the main landing station for trans-atlantic deep-Sea cables, the Museum of Submarine Telegraphy and a white beach formed from ground sea shells. To the east at Treryn Dinas Cliff Castle is The Logan Rock, a finely balanced 65 ton rock which used to rock easily until dislodged in 1824 by a Lieutenant Goldsmith, who later had to pay for it to be repositioned. Further round the coast is Mousehole, an attractive Cornish fishing harbour.

The Land's End peninsula abounds with prehistoric monuments. Among the more notable are Boscawen-un Stone Circle near St Buryan, with its 19 stones the most famous bronze age circle in Cornwall, Merry Maidens Stone Circle at Lamorna and Carn Euny Ancient Village at Sancreed. Lanyon Quoit, the hoop shaped Men-an-Tol, Men Scryfa Inscribed Stone and Nine Maidens Stone Circle are at Great Bosullow and the iron age Chysauster Ancient Village is near New Mill.

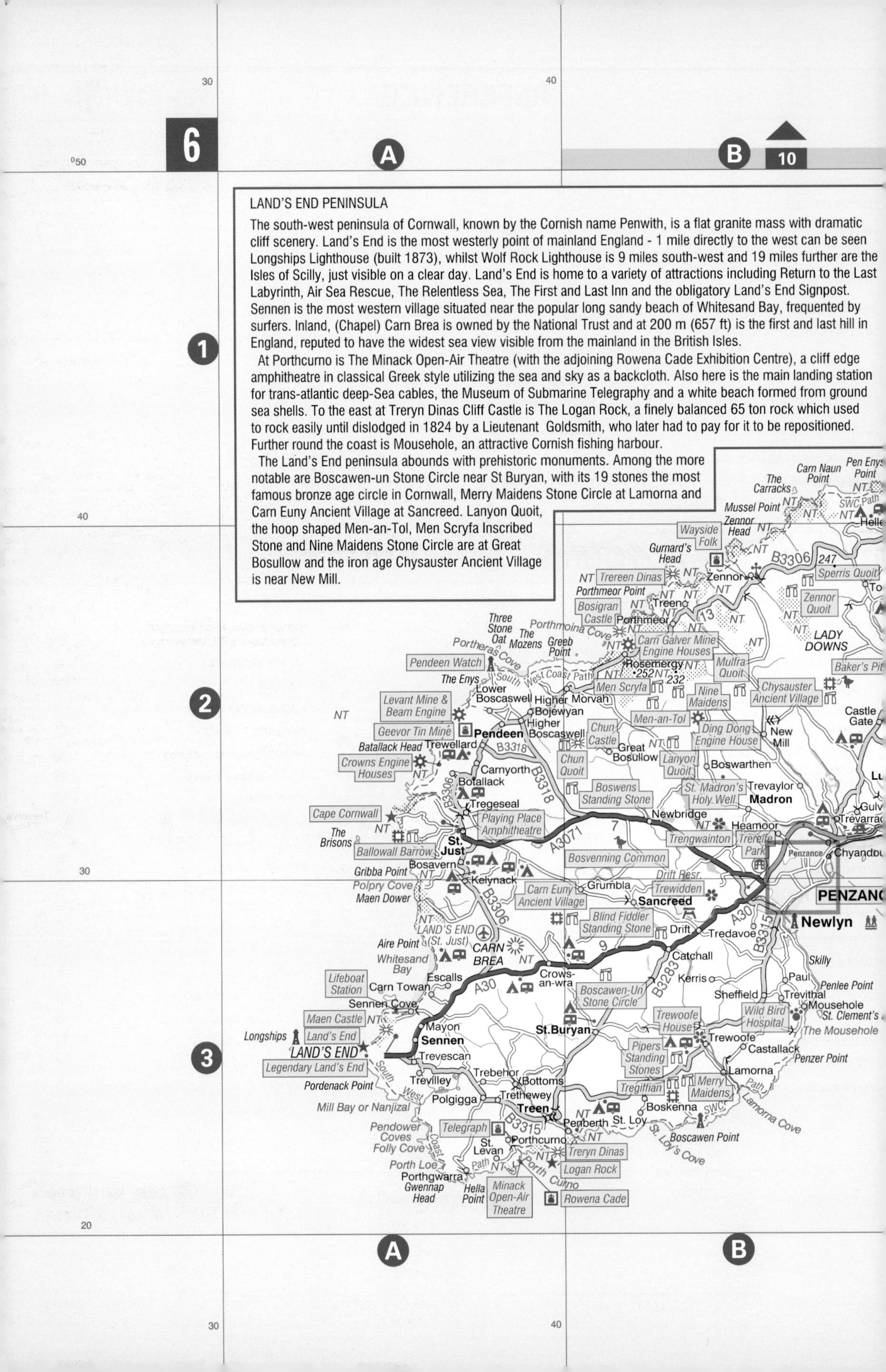

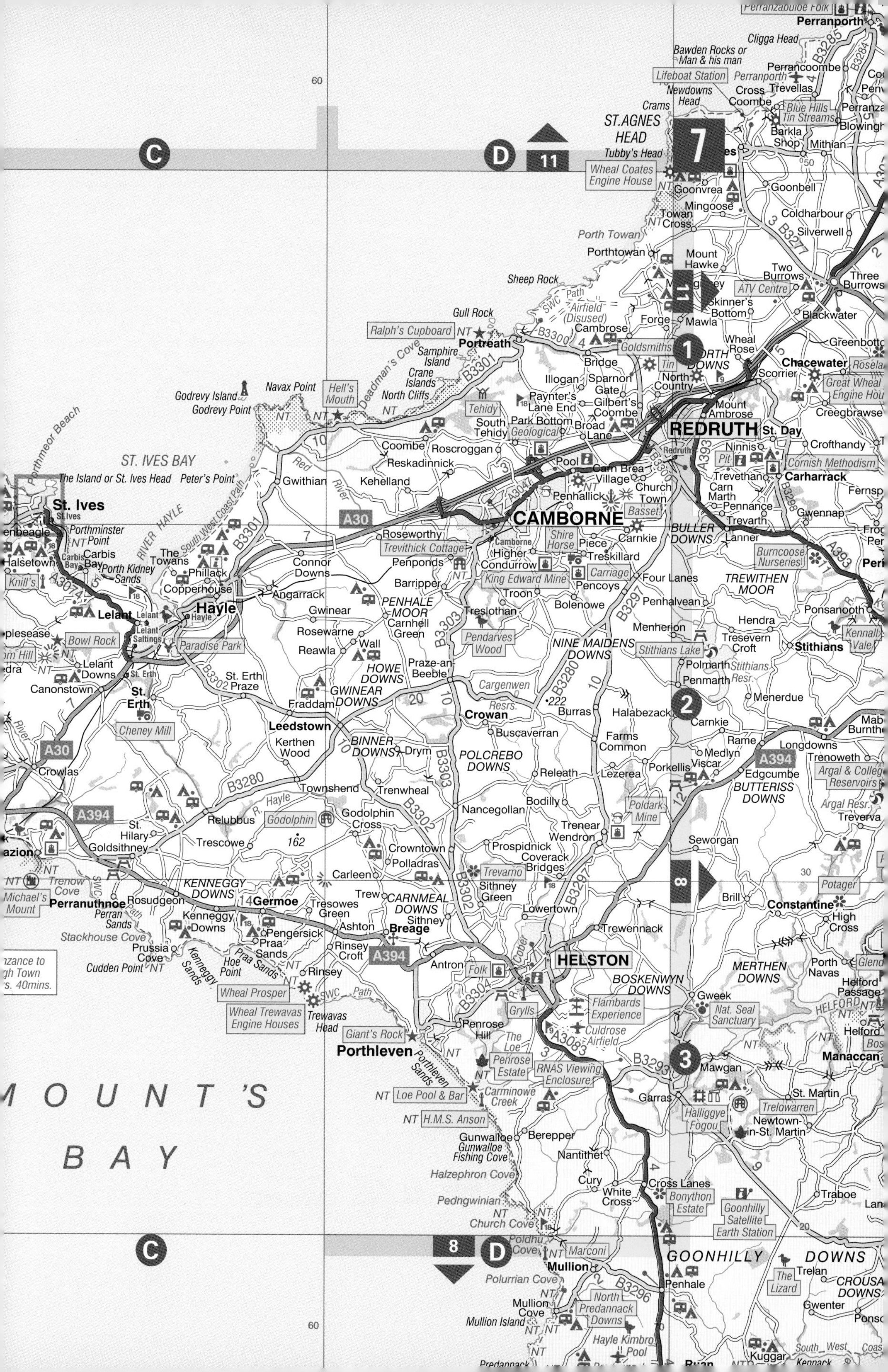

Perranzabuloe Folk
Perranporth
Cligga Head
Bawden Rocks or Man & his man
Perrancoombe
Lifeboat Station
Perranporth
Newdowns Head
Cross Coombe
Trevellas
Crams
ST. AGNES HEAD
Blue Hills Tin Streams
Perranza
Blowingh
Barkla Shop
Mithian
7
11
C
D
60
Tubby's Head
Wheal Coates Engine House
Goonvrea
Goonbell
Mingoose
Towan Cross
Coldharbour
Silverwell
Porth Towan
Porthtowan
Mount Hawke
Two Burrows
Three Burrows
Sheep Rock
ATV Centre
Skinner's Bottom
Airfield (Disused)
SWC Path
Mawla
Blackwater
Gull Rock
Forge
Cambrose
Ralph's Cupboard
Portreath
Goldsmiths
Wheal Rose
Greenbotto
Samphire Island
Crane Islands
North Cliffs
Deadman's Cove
Bridge
Tin
North Country
North Downs
Chacewater
Rosela
Scorrier
Great Wheal Engine Hou
Illogan
Sparnon Gate
Navax Point
Hell's Mouth
Godrevy Island
Godrevy Point
Tehidy
Paynter's Lane End
Gilbert's Coombe
Mount Ambrose
Creegbrawse
South Tehidy
Park Bottom
Geological
Broad Lane
REDRUTH
St. Day
Portmeor Beach
Coombe
Roscroggan
Reskadinnick
Ninnis
Crofthandy
Pool
Pit
Cornish Methodism
ST. IVES BAY
Red River
Cam Brea Village
Redruth
Trevethan
Carharrack
The Island or St. Ives Head
Peter's Point
Gwithian
Kehelland
Church Town
Carn Marth
Fernsp
Penhallick
Pennance
Gwennap
St. Ives
South West Coast Path
RIVER HAYLE
A30
CAMBORNE
Basset
Trevarth
Carnkie
BULLER DOWNS
Lanner
Frog
Per
Porthminster Point
Roseworthy
Camborne
Shire Horse
Piece
Trevithick Cottage
Burncoose Nurseries
Carbis Bay
The Towans
Connor Downs
Penponds
Higher Condurrow
Treskillard
Halsetown
Phillack
Porth Kidney Sands
Carriage
Four Lanes
TREWITHEN MOOR
Knill's
Copperhouse
Barripper
King Edward Mine
Pencoys
A3074
Angarrack
Troon
Bolenowe
Penhalvean
Ponsanooth
Lelant
Hayle
PENHALE MOOR
Gwinear
Treslothan
Hendra
Lelant Saltings
Paradise Park
Rosewarne
Carnhell Green
Menherion
Bowl Rock
Wall
Pendarves Wood
Tresevern Croft
Kennall Vale
Reawla
NINE MAIDENS DOWNS
Stithians Lake
Stithians
Lelant Downs
HOWE DOWNS
Praze-an-Beeble
Polmarth
Stithians Resr.
St. Erth
St. Erth Praze
Penmarth
Canonstown
GWINEAR DOWNS
Cargenwen Resrs.
Menerdue
Fraddam
Crowan
222
Burras
Halabezack
Carnkie
Leedstown
Buscaverran
Mab Burnth
Cheney Mill
Kerthen Wood
BINNER DOWNS
Drym
POLCREBO DOWNS
Farms Common
Rame
Longdowns
River
Medlyn
Trenoweth
A30
Crowlas
Releath
Lezerea
Porkellis
Viscar
A394
Edgcumbe
Argal & College Reservoirs
B3280
Townshend
Trenwheal
BUTTERISS DOWNS
Poldark Mine
R. Hayle
Argal Resr.
A394
Relubbus
Godolphin
Godolphin Cross
Nancegollan
Bodilly
Treverva
St. Hilary
Trenear
Wendron
Seworgan
Goldsithney
Trescowe
162
Crowntown
Prospidnick
Coverack Bridges
Polladras
Trevarno
Trenow Cove
30
Potager
Michael's Mount
Carleen
KENNEGGY DOWNS
Sithney Green
Perranuthnoe
Rosudgeon
Germoe
Trew
CARNMEAL DOWNS
Brill
Constantine
Perran Sands
Tresowes Green
Lowertown
High Cross
Stackhouse Cove
Kenneggy Downs
Sithney
Pengersick
Ashton
Breage
Trewennack
Praa Sands
Prussia Cove
Rinsey Croft
nzance to gh Town rs. 40mins.
Cudden Point
Kenneggy Sands
Hoe Point
Praa Sands
Rinsey
Antron
Folk
Cober
HELSTON
MERTHEN DOWNS
Porth Navas
Glend
BOSKENWYN DOWNS
Helford Passage
Wheal Prosper
Gweek
HELFORD
Flambards Experience
Wheal Trewavas Engine Houses
Trewavas Head
Gryls
Nat. Seal Sanctuary
Helford
Giant's Rock
Penrose Hill
The Loe
Culdrose Airfield
Porthleven
Porthleven Sands
Penrose Estate
RNAS Viewing Enclosure
Manaccan
Bos
MOUNT'S BAY
Mawgan
NT
Loe Pool & Bar
Carminowe Creek
Garras
St. Martin
Trelowarren
Halliggye Fogou
H.M.S. Anson
Newtown-in-St. Martin
Gunwalloe
Berepper
Gunwalloe Fishing Cove
Nantithet
Halzephron Cove
Cury
White Cross
Cross Lanes
Bonython Estate
Goonhilly Satellite Earth Station
Traboe
Lan
Pedngwinian
Church Cove
Poldhu Cove
Marconi
8
GOONHILLY DOWNS
Mullion
Penhale
The Lizard
Trelan
CROUSA DOWNS
Polurrian Cove
Mullion Cove
North Predannack Downs
Gwenter
Ponsc
Mullion Island
Hayle Kimbro Pool
Kuggar
South West Coast
Kennack
Predannack
Ruan
A394
A393
A3047
A3083
B3285
B3284
B3277
B3300
B3301
B3302
B3303
B3297
B3280
B3304
B3293
B3296

8
ST. IVES BAY
St. Ives Head
Peter's Point
Godrevy Island
Godrevy Point
Navax Point
Hell's Mouth
North Cliffs
Crane Islands
Deadman's Cove
Tehidy
South Tehidy
Geological
Paynter's Lane End
Park Bottom
Illogan
Sparnon Gate
Gilbert's Coombe
Broad Lane
North Country
Scorrier
Chacewater
Roseland House
Great Wheal Busy Engine Houses
Newbridge
Hugus
Mount Ambrose
REDRUTH
St. Day
Creegbrawse
Ninnis
Crofthandy
Twelveheads
Wheal Baddon
Pit
Cornish Methodism
Bissoe
Trevethan
Carharrack
Fernsplatt
Carn Marth
Pennance
Trevarth
11
B
Cusgarne
Coombe
Roscroggan
Reskadinnick
Kehelland
Pool
Carn Brea Village
Church Town
Penhallick
A
CAMBORNE
Basset
Red River
RIVER HAYLE
South West Coast Path
A30
B3301
Roseworthy
Trevithick Cottage
Shire Horse
Piece
Carnkie
BULLER DOWNS
Lanner
Burncoose Nurseries
Frogpool
Perranwell
Perranarworthal
The Towans
Phillack
Copperhouse
Connor Downs
Penponds
Higher Condurrow
Treskillard
Carriage
King Edward Mine
Four Lanes
TREWITHEN MOOR
Perran Wharf
Hayle
Angarrack
Barripper
Pencoys
Troon
Bolenowe
Penhalvean
Ponsanooth
Kennall Vale
A39
Lelant
Lelant Saltings
Paradise Park
Gwinear
Rosewarne
Reawla
Wall
PENHALE MOOR
Carnhell Green
Treslothan
B3303
Pendarves Wood
Menherion
Hendra
Tresevern Croft
Stithians
NINE MAIDENS DOWNS
Stithians Lake
Polmarth
Stithians Resr.
Enys
St. Erth
St. Erth Praze
B3302
HOWE DOWNS
Praze-an-Beeble
Cargenwen Resrs.
B3280
Penmarth
Menerdue
PENRYN
GWINEAR DOWNS
1
Leedstown
Crowan
Burras
Halabezack
Carnkie
Mabe Burnthouse
Cheney Mill
Kerthen Wood
BINNER DOWNS
Drym
Buscaverran
Farms Common
Rame
Longdowns
POLCREBO DOWNS
Medlyn
Trenoweth
Releath
Lezerea
Porkellis
Viscar
A394
Edgcumbe
College Resr.
Argal & College Reservoirs
BUTTERISS DOWNS
B3280
Townshend
Trenwheal
Hayle
Bodilly
Poldark Mine
Argal Resr.
Budock Water
Relubbus
Godolphin
Godolphin Cross
Nancegollan
Trevera
St. Hilary
Trescowe
162
Crowntown
Trenear
Wendron
Seworgan
Penjerrick
Prospidnick
Coverack Bridges
Polladras
Trevarno
KENNEGGY DOWNS
Carleen
Sithney Green
7
Potager
Bareppa
Rosudgeon
Germoe
Tresowes Green
Trew
CARNMEAL DOWNS
Sithney
Lowertown
Brill
Constantine
High Cross
Mawnan Smith
Carlidnack
Kenneggy Downs
Pengersick
Praa Sands
Ashton
Breage
Trewennack
Carwinion
Prussia Cove
Hoe Point
Kenneggy Sands
Rinsey Croft
Rinsey
A394
Antron
Folk
HELSTON
MERTHEN DOWNS
Porth Navas
Glendurgan
Durgan
Helford Passage
Trebah
Wheal Prosper
SWC Path
BOSKENWYN DOWNS
Gweek
HELFORD RIVER
Wheal Trewavas Engine Houses
Trewavas Head
Grylls
Flambards Experience
Nat. Seal Sanctuary
Helford
St. Anthony-in-Meneage
Giant's Rock
Penrose Hill
The Loe
Culdrose Airfield
A3083
Bosahan
Flushing
2
Porthleven
Porthleven Sands
Penrose Estate
RNAS Viewing Enclosure
B3293
Mawgan
Manaccan
Loe Pool & Bar
Carminowe Creek
Garras
St. Martin
H.M.S. Anson
Halliggye Fogou
Trelowarren
Newtown-in-St. Martin
Tregarne
Tregowris
MOUNT'S BAY
Gunwalloe
Gunwalloe Fishing Cove
Berepper
Nantithet
Halzephron Cove
Cury
White Cross
Cross Lanes
Bonython Estate
Goonhilly Satellite Earth Station
Traboe
Lanarth
Pedngwinian
Church Cove
Poldhu Cove
Marconi
20
Mullion
Polurrian Cove
GOONHILLY DOWNS
The Lizard
Trelan
CROUSA DOWNS
Coverack
Penhale
B3296
North Predannack Downs
Mullion Cove
Mullion Island
Gwenter
Ponsongath
B3294
Hayle Kimbro Pool
Predannack Airfield
Predannack Head
Ruan Major
Kuggar
Kennack Sands
South West Coast Path
Treleaver
Black Head
Poltesco
Carleon Cove
Spernic Cove
Pol Cornick
Ruan Pool
St. Ruan
Ruan Minor
Vellan Head
3
LIZARD DOWNS
Cadgwith
Devil's Frying Pan
The Horse
Kynance Cove
Grade
Devil's Bellows Blow-hole
Asparagus Island
Lizard
Bass Point
LIZARD POINT
Lizard
Lion's Den
Lizard Point
Polpeor Cove
10
A
B
60
70

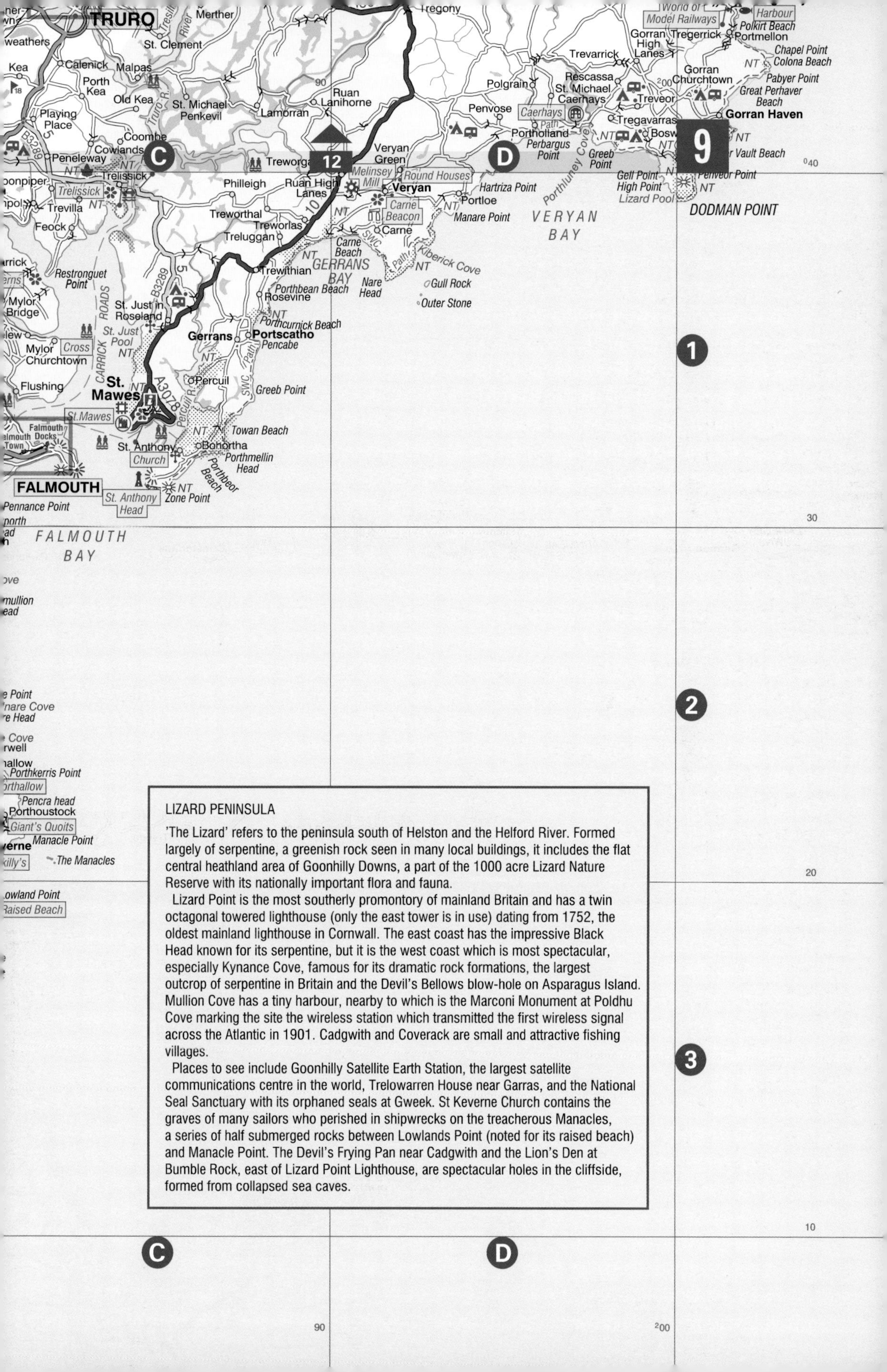

LIZARD PENINSULA

'The Lizard' refers to the peninsula south of Helston and the Helford River. Formed largely of serpentine, a greenish rock seen in many local buildings, it includes the flat central heathland area of Goonhilly Downs, a part of the 1000 acre Lizard Nature Reserve with its nationally important flora and fauna.

Lizard Point is the most southerly promontory of mainland Britain and has a twin octagonal towered lighthouse (only the east tower is in use) dating from 1752, the oldest mainland lighthouse in Cornwall. The east coast has the impressive Black Head known for its serpentine, but it is the west coast which is most spectacular, especially Kynance Cove, famous for its dramatic rock formations, the largest outcrop of serpentine in Britain and the Devil's Bellows blow-hole on Asparagus Island. Mullion Cove has a tiny harbour, nearby to which is the Marconi Monument at Poldhu Cove marking the site the wireless station which transmitted the first wireless signal across the Atlantic in 1901. Cadgwith and Coverack are small and attractive fishing villages.

Places to see include Goonhilly Satellite Earth Station, the largest satellite communications centre in the world, Trelowarren House near Garras, and the National Seal Sanctuary with its orphaned seals at Gweek. St Keverne Church contains the graves of many sailors who perished in shipwrecks on the treacherous Manacles, a series of half submerged rocks between Lowlands Point (noted for its raised beach) and Manacle Point. The Devil's Frying Pan near Cadgwith and the Lion's Den at Bumble Rock, east of Lizard Point Lighthouse, are spectacular holes in the cliffside, formed from collapsed sea caves.

10
A
B
1
2
3
6
7
ST. IVES BAY
St. Ives
Hayle
Lelant
Zennor
Godrevy Island
Godrevy Point
Navax Point
Porthmeor Beach
The Island or St. Ives Head
Peter's Point
The Carracks
Carn Naun Point
Pen Enys Point
Hor Point
Mussel Point
Zennor
Wayside Folk
Gurnard's Head
Trereen Dinas
Porthmeor Point
Bosigran Castle
Porthmeor
Treen
Three Stone Oat
The Mozens
Greeb Point
Porthmoina Cove
Carn Galver Mine Engine Houses
Hellesveor
Penbeagle
Halsetown
Porthminster Point
Carbis Bay
Porth Kidney Sands
Bussow Res.
Knill's
Sperris Quoit
Zennor Quoit
Towednack
LADY DOWNS
Cripplesease
Bowl Rock
Lelant Saltings
The Towans
Phillack
Copperhouse
Paradise Park
Angarrack
Gwithian
South West Coast Path
SWC Path
B3306
B3301
A3074

11
70
80
C
D
Treyarnon Point
Treyarnon
Fox Cove
Porthcothan Bay
Porthcothan
High Cove
Park Head
Bedruthan Steps
High Cove
Trenance Point
Trenance
Mawgan Porth
Berryl's Point
Beacon Cove
Trevarrian
Strasse Cliff
Watergate Bay
Tregurrian
Zacry's Island
Trevelgue Head
Towan Head
Newquay Bay
Porth
St. Columb Minor
NEWQUAY
Newquay
Pentire Point East
Pentire Point West
Pentire
West Pentire
Kelsey Head
Crantock
Trencreek
Chapel
Quintrel Downs
A3058
A392
Lane
Trevemper
Quintrell Downs
Holywell Bay
Carter's or Gull Rocks
Trevowah
Fun Park
Penhale Point
Holywell
Tresean
Treveal
Gwills
Kestle
Trerice
Hoblyn's Cove
Ligger Point
Penhale Camp
Cubert
A3075
12
Trevoll
Benny Halt
Benny Mill
Gummow's Shop
Penhale Sands
Ligger or Perran Bay
Perran Beach
St. Piran's Oratory
St. Newlyn East
Rejerrah
Lappa Valley Steam Railway
Treamble
East Wheal Rose
Trevilson
Gear Sands
Newlyn Halt
Lappa Valley
Cotty's Point
Rose
Fiddlers Green
Perranzabuloe Folk
St. Piran's
Shepherds
NEWLYN DOWNS
Perranporth
Cligga Head
B3285
Goonhavern
A39
Bawden Rocks or Man & his man
Bolingey
Lifeboat Station
Perranporth
Perrancoombe
Perranwell
World in Miniature
B3284
Newdowns Head
Cross Coombe
Trevellas
Cocks
Penwartha
Wheal Frances
Zelah
Crams
ST.AGNES HEAD
Blue Hills Tin Streams
Perranzabuloe
Blowinghouse
Ventongimps
Higher Bal
Barkla Shop
Mithian
Penhallow
St. Allen
Tubby's Head
St. Agnes
Callestick
Marazanvose
Trispen
Wheal Coates Engine House
Goonvrea
Cyder Farm
St. Erme
7
Goonbell
Tresawsen
Mingoose
Towan Cross
Coldharbour
Allet
Idless Wood
B3277
Porth Towan
Silverwell
A30
Porthtowan
Mount Hawke
Little Croft West
Shortlanesend
Idless
Two Burrows
Three Burrows
Roseworthy
Sheep Rock
Menagissey
ATV Centre
SWC Path
Airfield (Disused)
Skinner's Bottom
Blackwater
Buckshead
Gull Rock
Mawla
Langarth
Kenwyn
Ralph's Cupboard
Portreath
Cambrose
Forge
A390
New Mill
Goldsmiths
Wheal Rose
Greenbottom
Truro
Samphire Island
Bridge
Tin
NORTH DOWNS
Chacewater
Roseland House
Threemilestone
Higher-town
TRURO
Deadman's Cove
Crane Islands
B3301
Illogan
Sparnon Gate
North Country
Scorrier
Great Wheal Busy Engine Houses
Newbridge
North Cliffs
Tehidy
Paynter's Lane End
Gilbert's Coombe
Mount Ambrose
Hugus
Penweathers
St. Clement
South Tehidy
Park Bottom
Geological
Broad Lane
REDRUTH
St. Day
Creegbrawse
Kea
Calenick
Malpas
Coombe
Roscroggan
Redruth
Crofthandy
Twelveheads
Porth Kea
Reskadinnick
Pool
Carn Brea Village
Ninnis
Wheal Baddon
Old Kea
B3300
A393
Pit
Cornish Methodism
Kehelland
A3047
Church Town
Trevethan
Carharrack
Bissoe
Helston Water
Playing Place
Penhallick
Carn Marth
Fernsplatt
Coombe
A30
CAMBORNE
Basset
Pennance
B3298
Gwennap
Cusgarne
Carnon Downs
Cowlands
Peneleway
Trelissick
Roseworthy
Shire Horse
Carnkie
BULLER DOWNS
Trevarth
Lanner
8
Frogpool
Perranwell
Goonpiper
Trevithick Cottage
Piece
Treskillard
Burncoose Nurseries
Devoran
Trelissick
Penponds
Condurrow
Perranarworthal
Penpol
Trevilla
King Edward Mine
Carriage
Four Lanes
TREWITHEN MOOR
Barripper
Pencoys
Perran Wharf
Carclew
Feock
Troon
Burncoose Nurseries
PENHALE MOOR
Bolenowe
Penhalvean
Carnhell Green
Treslothan
Ponsanooth
B3303
B3297
Hendra
Angarrick
Restronguet Point
Menherion
Kennall Vale
Lanterns
Pendarves Wood
NINE MAIDENS DOWNS
Stithians Lake
Tresevern Croft
Stithians
A39
B3289
Wall

12
18
9
A
B
1
2
3
70
80
90
60
Treyarnon Point
Treyarnon
Towan
Harlyn
B3276
St. Merryn
Dinas
RIVER
Cant Hill
Cant Cove
CAMEL
Treworhan
Tregonce
Camel Trail
Tregunna
Trevanson
A389
Fox Cove
Shop
Porthcothan Bay
Little Petherick
Edmonton
Whitecross
Trevance
St. Breock
St. Issey
Porthcothan
Old Macdonald's Farm
St. Merryn
Mellingey Mill
Ryl. Cornwall Showground
High Cove
Park Head
Penrose
Trenance
Tredinnick
Hawke's Wood
Burlawn
Treburrick
Rumford
St. Ervan
Trelow
St. Jidgey
Pawton Quoit
Bedruthan Steps
ST. BREOCK DOWNS
Downhill Meadow
Crealy
B3274
B3276
TRELOW DOWNS
The Fiddler
Monolith
ROSENANNON DOWNS
High Cove
Trenance Point
St. Eval
Trenance
Trevilledor
Lower Lanherne
DENZELL DOWNS
Mawgan Porth
Berryl's Point
Beacon Cove
Gluvian
Nine Maidens Stone Row
Japanese
Winnard's Perch
Trevarrian
St. Mawgan
Cornish Birds of Prey Centre
Retallack
Rosenannon
Strasse Cliff
Rosedinnick
Westworld Raceway
Spirit of The West
St. Wenn
Withiel
Watergate Bay
Tregurrian
Talskiddy
SWC Path
R. Menalhyl
Gluvian
NEWQUAY
Tregamere
B3274
Tregonetha
Demelza
Zacry's Island
St. Columb Major
A3059
Trevelgue Head
Tregaswith
Tregatillian
CASTLE DOWNS
Belowda Beacon
227
Towan Head
Newquay Bay
Porth
St. Columb Minor
Porth Resr.
Trekenning
Castle-an-Dinas
214
Belowda
NEWQUAY
Springfields Fun Park
Pentire Point East
Pentire
Newquay
Trencreek
A3058
Trebudannon
Pentire Point West
West Pentire
Chapel
Colan
A39
Screech Owl Sanctuary
Kelsey Head
Crantock
Lane
Quintrel Downs
Mountjoy
Bosoughan
Black Cross
Ruthvoes
Tregoss
A392
A392
Trevarren
Holywell Bay
Trevemper
Quintrell Downs
Cornwall Pearl
White Cross
Toldish
GOSS MOOR
Roche Rock
Carter's or Gull Rocks
Trevowah
St. Columb Road
St. Columb Road
A30
Enniscaven
Penhale Point
Fun Park
R. Gannel
Gwills
Kestle Mill
Indian Queens
Carne
Coldvreath
Gothers
Holywell
Tresean
Trerice
Dairyland Farm World
Fraddon
Hoblyn's Cove
Treveal
Blue Anchor
Cleers
Ligger Point
Penhale Camp
Trevoll
Gummow's Shop
Troan
St. Dennis
Whitemoor
A3075
Benny Halt
Benny Mill
Penhale
Hendra
Hensbarrow
Penhale Sands
St. Enoder
B3279
Perran Beach
St. Newlyn East
Lappa Valley Steam Railway
A3058
Curnan Vale
Ligger or Perran Bay
St. Piran's Oratory
Rejerrah
East Wheal Rose
A3076
Summercourt
Treviscoe
Nanpean
Treamble
Trevilson
Greensplat
Gear Sands
Hendra Croft
Newlyn Halt
Lappa Valley
Chapel Town
B3275
Melbur
Trethosa
Cotty's Point
Rose
Fiddlers Green
Scarcewater
Foxhole
St. Piran
Shepherds
NEWLYN DOWNS
Mitchell
Brighton
Menna
R. Fal
Carpalla
Perranporth
Goonhavern
Tregargus
Terras
Hornick
B3285
Bolingey
B3285
High Street
A39
A3058
St. Stephen
Gwindra
Lanjeth
Trewoon
Cocks
Perranwell
World in Miniature
Trelassick
Penwartha
Wheal Frances
Trendeal
Trelion
Perranzabuloe
Ventongimps
Zelah
New Mills
St. Mewan
Blowinghouse
Coombe
Penhallow
St. Allen
Tregear
Ladock
Mithian
Marazanvose
Trispen
Grampound Road
Downderry
Callestick
Cyder Farm
A390
Tresawsen
St. Erme
River Fal
Sticker
Hewas Water
Paramoor
Allet
Idless Wood
Grampound
Tortoise Garden
A30
Shortlanesend
B3284
Probus
Trewithen
Rescoria
Little Croft West
Idless
Trewithen
Three Burrows
Roseworthy
A39
B3275
Trelowthas
Creed
Creed House
Lost Gardens of Heligan
Buckshead
A390
Blackwater
Tresillian
Langarth
A390
Kenwyn
Tresawle
B3287
St. Ewe
New Mill
Tucoyse
Greenbottom
Truro
Pencalenick
Polmassick
Polmassick
Roseland House
Threemilestone
A3078
Tregony
Great Wheal Busy Engine Houses
Newbridge
Higher-town
TRURO
Tresillian River
Merther
Hugus
Penweathers
St. Clement
Creegbrawse
Calenick
Malpas
Kea
Trevarrick
Porth Kea
Crofthandy
Twelveheads
Rescassa
Wheal Baddon
Old Kea
Truro R.
St. Michael Penkevil
Ruan Lanihorne
Polgrain
St. Michael Caerhays
Cornish Methodism
Bissoe
Helston Water
Lamorran
Penvose
Caerhays
Tregavarras
Carnon
Playing Place
Fernsplatt
Carnon Downs
B3289
Coombe
Portholland
Veryan Green
Perbargus Point
Greeb Point
Cusgarne
Cowlands
Gwennap
Peneleway
R. Fal
Treworga
Porthluney Cove
Frogpool
Perranwell
Trelissick
Melinsey Mill
Round Houses
Gell Point
High Point
Lizard Point
Perranwell
Goonpiper
Devoran
Trelissick
Philleigh
Ruan Lanes
Veryan
Portloe
Perranarworthal
Penpol
Trevilla
Carne Beacon
Manare Point
VERYAN BAY
Treworthal
Treworlas
Feock
Perran Wharf
Treluggan
Carne
Carclew
Carne Beach
Kiberick Cove
Ponsanooth
Kennal
GERRANS BAY
Angarrick
Trewithian
Gull Rock
Restronguet Point
Nare Head
Lanterns
A39
B3289
Porthbean Beach
Stithians
Kennall Vale
Rosevine
A393

To the Keeper of the Gate

To my well beloved friend, Greetings!

Sir, I beseech thee to welcome and protect the bearer of this letter, whom I commend to thee.
Pray, let thine warders and servants give the bearer all accord, shelter and protection from the murderers, thieves, ruffians and spirits that abide in this establishment.
I also confirm that the bearer is a suitable person to be allowed to visit the Jail Tavern to partake of food and ale at a fair price.

Your most humble servant and friend,

James Chapple

Governor of Bodmin Jail
In the Year of our Lord 1779

Wadebridge
St.Mabyn
Longstone
Blisland
Waterloo
Penpont
Jubilee Rock
Trippet Stone Circle
Reservoir
Dozmary Pool
Colliford Lake
COLLIFORD LAKE
Temple
BLACKTOR DOWNS
Browngelly Downs
Settlements
Brown Gelly Barrows
Stowe's Pound
The Cheesewring
Stone Circle
Siblyback Lake
Hurlers Stone Circles
Minions
TWELVE MEN'S MOOR
Old Mill Herbary
Hellandbridge
Helland
Pencarrow
Sladesbridge
Croanford
Camel Trail
A389
B3266
CARDINHAM MOOR
Maidenwell
Warleggan
Millpool
Bury Castle
13
19
Washaway
Camel Valley
Brocton
Boscarne
Boscarne Junction
Bodiniel
Dunmere
Cooksland
Cardinham
Cross
Treslea
Mount
Warleggan
Fawton
St. Neot Holy Well
St.Neot
Pantersbridge
Lampen
Treverbyn
Draynes
Golitha Falls
Trenant
Redgate
King Doniert's Stone
Trethevy Quoit
St. Cleer
Common Moor
Cardinham Castle
Cardinham Woods
Rutherbridge
Nanstallon
St. Lawrence
Bodmin
Bodmin General
Withielgoose Mills
Fletchersbridge
Colesloggett Halt
Pinsla
Carnglaze Slate Caverns
Tredinnick
Ley
John Southern Gallery
Coldwind
Dobwalls
Doublebois
Liskeard & District
Trembraze
Bodmin & Wenford
B3268
A38
A30
Tremore
Lamorick
Tregullon
Lanivet
Cutmadoc
Bodmin Parkway
Middle Taphouse
East Taphouse
Trevelmond
Ancient Egyptian
Moorswater
Viaduct
Lamellion
Coombe
Trebyan
Lanhydrock
Bofarnel
Lanhydrock Estate
West Taphouse
A390
Braddock
Bokiddick
Sweetshouse
Restormel
Lockengate
Redmoor
Breney Common
B3269
B3359
Boconnoc House & Garden
Boconnoc
Polscoe
Bodwen
Lostwithiel
Herodsfoot
St. Keyne
St.Keyne
St. Keyne Holy Well
Magnificent Music Machines
Porfell Animal Land
Couch's Mill
Bugle
Lanlivery
Lostwithiel
Herodsfoot Woods
Causeland
Duloe
Churchbridge
Stone Circle
Rosevean
Luxulyan
Luxulyan Bridges
Bocaddon
Folk & Farm
Lanreath
Tregarne Mill
Tredinnick
Wringworthy
Tregarland
Rescorla
Treffry Viaduct
Farm
St.Winnow
Lerryn
R. Lerryn
Treverbyn
Resugga Green
Hidden Valley
Muchlarnick
Sandplace
Penpillick
Penwithick
Carthew
Trethurgy
Tywardreath Highway
Hall Rings
Pelynt
Ruddlemoor
Eden Project
Garker
Tregrehan Mills
St.Blazey
St.Blazey Gate
Marsh Villa
Tywardreath
Torfrey
Golant
Cliff
St.Veep
Penpoll
Great Tree
Carclaze
ST. AUSTELL
Boscoppa
Bethel
Holmbush
Tregrehan
Par
Biscovey
A3082
Castle Dore
Lanteglos Highway
Trenewan
Kilminorth Woods
West Looe
A387
Polmear
Par Sands
Fowey
R. FOWEY
Mixtow
Bodinnick
Pont
Portlooe
Porthallow
Bens Play World
Carlyon Bay
Charlestown
Tristan Stone
Polruan
Lansallos
Polperro
Crumplehorn
Talland Bay
Portnadler Bay
Duporth
Shipwreck & Heritage
Tregorrick
ST. AUSTELL BAY
Lantivet Bay
S.W. Coast Path
Higher Porthpean
Square Sail Shipyard
London Apprentice
Little Gribbin
Daymark
Southground Point
Pencarrow Head
Colors Cove
Land of Legend & Model Village
Smuggling & Fishing
Phoebe's Point
Gwendra Point
Ropehaven Cliffs
Levalsa Meor
Trenarren
Hallane
GRIBBIN HEAD
Sandy Cove
Black Head
Pentewan
Pentewan Beach
MEVAGISSEY BAY
Penare Point
Polstreath
Folk
Mevagissey
Harbour
Polkirt Beach
Portmellon
Chapel Point
Colona Beach
Pabyer Point
Great Perhaver Beach
Gorran Haven
Bow or Vault Beach
Penveor Point
DODMAN POINT
NT
C
D
1
2
3
14
10
20
40

Reservoir
Dozmary Pool
TWELVE MEN'S MOOR
Botternell
Bathpool
Bray Shop
Climsland
Lidwell
Old Mill
Colliford Lake
COLLIFORD LAKE
Temple
BLACKTOR DOWNS
Browngelly Downs
342
Settlements
327
344
Henwood
North Darley
Linkinhorne
Millcombe
B3257
Darleyford
Cheese Farm
Rilla Mill
Netherton
Stowe's Pound
Rillaton Barrow
The Cheesewring
Upton
Theatre
Sutton
Plushabridge
South Hill
Mornick
Downgate
Brown Gelly Barrows
Warleggan R.
255
265
272
Stone Circle
Upton Cross
Caradon Town
Trewoodloe
Maders
Kelly Bray
Phoenix United Mine
Siblyback Lake
Hurlers Stone Circle
Minions
Downgate
Golberdon
A388
Kit Hill
14
277
A
Sth. Phoenix Mine
20
B
Hayes
Bowling Green
Rising Sun
Siblyback Lake
Common Moor
Higher Tremarcoombe
Trevigro
Callington
Harrowbarrow
70
Warleggan
Draynes
King Doniert's Stone
Darite
Crow's Nest
Pensilva
Callington
Dupath Holy Well
Golitha Falls
Trethevy Quoit
Tremar
Middlehill
Ken-Caro
Fawton
St. Neot Holy Well
Redgate
Woolston
Gang
Frogwell
Mount
St.Neot
Trenant
St. Cleer
Keason
Castlewich Henge
Ashton
Pantersbridge
Treverbyn
St. Cleer Holy Well
Newbridge
Lampen
St. Ive
Cadson Bury
Parkfield
NT
Bealbury
Carnglaze Slate Caverns
John Southern Gallery
B3254
Tredinnick
Ley
R. Fowey
Merrymeet
Pillaton Clapper
A390
Coldwind
Dobwalls
Trembraze
Hendrabridge
St. Mellion
12
1
Dobwalls
Liskeard & District
Doublebois
Dobwalls
Ancient Egyptian
Addington
Pengover Green
Quethiock
6
Liskeard
River Lynher
Pillaton
Paynter's Cross
Middle Taphouse
East Taphouse
Moorswater
Viaduct
Trevelmond
Liskeard
Trehunist
West Taphouse
Coombe
Lamellion
Trewint
Holwood
Pillatonmill
Sillaton
Blunts
R. Tiddy
Lake
Menheniot
Doddycross
Cuttivett
Braddock
Magnificent Music Machines
St. Keyne
Menheniot
Tilland
Tideford Cross
Brighton
Notter
St.Keyne
Landrake
Boconnoc
B3359
Herodsfoot
Horningtops
Cutmere
60
Porfell Animal Land
St. Keyne Holy Well
A38
Budge's Shop
Trewidland
A38
Trematon
Couch's Mill
B3252
Tideford
Herodsfoot Woods
R. Seaton
Causeland
Catchfrench Manor
Kernow Mill
St. Erney
Markwell
R. Lerryn
W. Looe R.
Churchbridger
Duloe
Trenode
Treruleofoot
B3249
Bocaddon
Stone Circle
Wringworthy
Widegates
Priory Church
Tregarland
Shortacross
A387
St.Germans
St. Germans
Folk & Farm
13
Tregarrick Mill
Tredinnick
A374
Hessenford
Lerryn
Lanreath
Muchlarnick
Morval
Sandplace
Sandplace
Trelowia
Polbathick
B3247
B3359
Hall Rings
B3253
Seaton Country Park
Narkurs
Cornish Owl Centre
Great Tree
St.Veep
2
Pelynt
St. Martin
St. Winnolls
Tredrossel
Sheviock
Crafthole
Scraesdon
Penpoll
Kilminorth Woods
Looe
Seaton
Keveral Beach
Trenewan
West Looe
Monkey Sanctuary
Downderry
The Long Stone
Portwrinkle
A387
Looe
Seaton Beach
Looe Bay
DANGER AREA
Long Sands
Portlooe
Porthallow
Hannafore Point
Sharrow Grotto
Pont
Crumplehorn
St. George's or Looe Island
WHITSAND BAY
Lansallos
S.W. Coast Path
Polperro
Talland Bay
Lantivet Bay
Portnadler Bay
Pencarrow Head
Colors Cove
Land of Legend & Model Village
Smuggling & Fishing
3
40
A
B
20
30

Three Oaks
Latchley
Abbey
TAVISTOCK
Moorshop
Moortown
Merrivale Settlement
Dartmoor Prison
Princetown
Dartmoor Prison
New Bridge
Chilsworthy
B3362
A390
Whitchurch
Brook
Middlemoor
Sampford Spiney
High Moorland
Tor Royal
Royal Hill
407
Hexworthy
Gunnislake
St. Ann's Chapel
B3257
Grenofen
Strane R.
R. Swincombe
Whiteworks
15
Copper
Drakewalls
C
21
Horrabridge
D
Albaston
Tamar Valley
Morwellham Quay
A386
Walkhampton
70
Norris Green
Calstock
Pinetum
Cotehele
Mill
NT
Buckland Monachorum
Garden House
Harrowbeer
B3212
Dousland
Burrator Reservoir
Burrator Reservoir
471 Crane Hill
Naker's Hill
Letterbox
Quay
Tuckermarsh
Crapstone
Axtown
Yelverton
Sheepstor
Bohetherick
Bere Alston
Buckland Abbey
Meavy
Stall Moor Stone Row
Red Lake
Clapper
CORNWALL
DEVON
Milton Combe
Ringmoor Down
Upper Plym Valley Prehistoric Sites
Hoo Meavy
R. Tavy
Langcombe Hill
Cotts
Clearbrook
Weir Quay
R. Plym
1
LEE MOOR
STALL MOOR
Tamar Belle Heritage Centre
Dewerstone Rock
Shaugh Prior
PENN MOOR
Bere Ferrers
Bere Ferrers
HARFORD MOOR
UGBOROUGH MOOR
Cargreen
RIVER TAMAR
R. TAVY
Roborough
Bickleigh
Landulph
Tamerton Foliot
A386
Lee Moor
Wotter
Rook Tor
Saltash
Tamar Estuary
Warleigh Point
Woolwell
Carkeel
Heritage Museum
Budshead Wood
Whitleigh
B3373
Crownhill Fort
B3432
Boringdon Camp
Royal Albert
Ernesettle
Whitleigh Wood
PLYMOUTH CITY
Bircham Valley
Cornwood
R. Erme
Burraton
TOLL
Estover
Crownhill
Cann Wood
B3417
Drakeland Corner
Lutton
Harford
Woodland Wood
Forder Valley
Hanger Down
Newman's Cottage
St. Budeaux
B3413
Plym Bridge
Yondertown
229
364
St. Stephens
Victoria Rd.
Ferry Rd.
Eggbuckland
Leigham
Dartmoor
Sparkwell
Lukesland
Ham
Penny-cross
Longbridge
Piers
Hemerdon Ho.
Efford Marshes
Hemerdon
16
Henlake Down
Antony Woodland
Plym Valley
Higher Compton
Woodford
Venton
212
Ivybridge
Antony
Keyham
B3416
Viaduct
Wilcove
PLYMOUTH
Chaddlewood
Maryfield
B3396
Plympton
Dockyard
Ford
Devonport
Lee Mill
A374
Stoke
Plymouth
B3214
Underwood
Devonport
Plympton
Torpoint
Devonport
Saltram
2
A38
HAMOAZE
Hardwick Wood
A38
Keaton
Deadman's Point
Scott Memorial
A379
Billacombe
Cattedown
Penquit
Penhale
Cremyll
The Hoe
Oreston
Westlake
South-down
Insworke
Turnchapel
Plymstock
Drake's Island
Ermington
Millbrook
Mount Edgcumbe
THE SOUND
Hooe
Elburton
Brixton
Yealmpton
Goosewell
A379
Tregonhawke
CAWSAND BAY
Staddon Point
Staddiscombe
Spriddlestone
Torr
Dunstone
Kingsand
Hollacombe Woods
Cawsand
Plymouth Breakwater
Andurn Point
Down Thomas
Holbeton
Luson
(Seasonal)
R. YEALM
B3186
50
Rame
Pier Cellars
Knighton
Heybrook Bay
Collaton
South West Coast Path
Wembury
Lillery's Cove
Penlee Point
Wembury Marine Conservation Area
The Old Mill
Marine Centre
Newton Ferrers
Great Torr
Battisborough Cross
RAME HEAD
Wembury Bay
Bridgend
Kingston
Mothecombe
B3392
Great Mew Stone
Noss Mayo
Gara Point
Coast Path
Scobbiscombe
Plymouth to:
Roscoff 6hrs.
Santander 20hrs. 30mins.
(Seasonal)
Blackstone Point
Hilsea Point
Stoke Beach
Stoke Point
Butcher's Cove
Beacon Point
Ringmore
3
Westcombe Beach
Challaborough
Bigbury-on-Sea
Burgh Island
BIGBURY BAY
Butter Cove
Thurlestone
40
BOLT
Redrot
C
D
250
60

16
A
HOLNE MOOR
22
B
Princetown
Dartmoor Prison
Merrivale Settlement
High Moorland
Tor Royal
Royal Hill
Whiteworks
Hexworthy
Huccaby
Dartmeet
Clapper
Corndon Tor
Ponsworthy
Leusdon
Blackadon
Buckland in the Moor
Lower Town
Poundsgate
Ten Commandments Stone
Dart Valley
Venford Reservoir
Sigford
Caton
Goodstone
St Lawrence Chapel
Hele
Ashburton
Knowle
Tree
Holne
Michelcombe
Scorriton
River Dart Adventures
Hembury Castle
Abbey
Buckfast
The Valiant Soldier
Buckfastleigh
BUCKFASTLEIGH MOOR
DEAN MOOR
Burrator Reservoir
Dousland
Sheepstor
Ringmoor Down
Upper Plym Valley Prehistoric Sites
Crane Hill
Naker's Hill
Letterbox
Stall Moor Stone Row
Red Lake
Clapper
Langcombe Hill
LEE MOOR
PENN MOOR
STALL MOOR
Avon Dam Reservoir
Rider's Rings Enclosures
BRENT MOOR
HARFORD MOOR
UGBOROUGH MOOR
Dewerstone Rock
Shaugh Prior
Lee Moor
Wotter
Rook Tor
Corringdon Ball Long Barrow
Didworthy
Lutton
Aish
South Brent
Hillside
Higher Dean
Lower Dean
South Devon Railway
Dean Prior
Harbourneford
Pennywell
Staverton
Cider Press Centre
Dartington
Rattery
Culverlane
Tigley
Totnes
Costume
Forder Green
Thornecroft
Landscove
Woolston Green
Railway
Butterfly and Otter
Hill House
Cornwood
Harford
Butterdon Stone Row
Butterdon Hill
Cheston
Hanger Down
Henlake Down
Lukesland
Bittaford
Ivybridge
Viaduct
Drakeland Corner
Lutton
Yondertown
Cann Wood
Dartmoor
Hemerdon Ho.
Hemerdon
Sparkwell
15
Chaddlewood
Lee Mill
Horsebrook
Avonwick
Langford Barton
Diptford
North Huish
West Leigh
Harberton
Ugborough
Keaton
Penquit
Westlake
Ermington
Curtisknowle
Boreston
Halwell
Lupridge
Moreleigh
Brownston
East Leigh
Hazelwood
Blackdown Rings
Andrew's Wood
Brixton
Yealmpton
Torr
Dunstone
Modbury
Holbeton
Luson
Collaton
Newton Ferrers
Battisborough Cross
Mothecombe
Bridgend
Noss Mayo
Great Torr
Kingston
St Ann's Chapel
Waterhead
Ford
Bridge End
Aveton Gifford
Ashford
Loddiswell
Woodleigh
East Allington
Venn
Sorley Tunnel
Churchstow
Ledstone
Goveton
Rimpston
Buckland-Tout-Saints
Cookworthy
Kingsbridge
Sherford
Frittiscombe
Woodford
Hutcherleigh
Scobbiscombe
Bigbury
Ringmore
Stoke Beach
Stoke Point
Butcher's Cove
Beacon Point
Westcombe Beach
Challaborough
Bigbury-on-Sea
Burgh Island
Bolberry Donkey Stud
West Buckland
East Buckland
Butter Cove
Thurlestone
BIGBURY BAY
Warren Point
South Milton
Sutton
West Alvington
Summer only
East Charleton
West Charleton
Frogmore
Chillington
Woolston
KINGSBRIDGE ESTUARY
Salcombe to Kingsbridge
Kernborough
South Pool
Beacon Point
Galmpton
Outer Hope
Inner Hope
BOLT TAIL
Redrot Cove
Malborough
Batson
Maritime
Collaton
Bolberry
Salcombe
East Portlemouth
Chivelstone
South Allington
Rew
Slippery Point
Soar
RNLI
Rickham
Soar Mill Cove
Overbeck's
Sharp Tor
Starehole
A38
A3121
A379
A381
A384
A385
B3196
B3213
B3372
B3392
B3194
B3186
B3417
B3212
B3357
1
2
3

Trago Mills
Teigngrace
Kingsteignton
Bishopsteignton
Rural Life
Sprey Point
Teignmouth
Teignmouth & Shaldon
Grand Pier
Lifeboat Station
Wildlife Trust
Gorse Blossom
Orchid Paradise
South Knighton
Mile End
Highweek
NEWTON ABBOT
Hackney Marshes
TEIGN
Shaldon
Ringmore
Combeinteignhead
Stokeinteignhead
17
West Ogwell
East Ogwell
Wolborough
Prickly Ball Farm (Hedgehog Hospital)
Decoy
Plant World
23
A380
Middle Rocombe
Lower Gabwell
Higher Gabwell
BABBACOMBE BAY
Maidencombe
Watcombe Head
Abbotskerswell
Denbury
Pleasant View Nursery
Two Mile Oak
Coffinswell
Kingskerswell
Daccombe
Torbryan
Ipplepen
Dainton
North Whilborough
Combe Pafford
Model Village
Bygones
Oddicombe Cliff Railway
Babbacombe
Anstey's Cove
Black Head
Kents Cavern
Edginswell
Shiphay
Combe Fishacre
Compton
Cockington Court
Craft Centre
Chelston
Torre
Cockington
Marldon
Occombe Farm Project
Littlehempston
Afton
Churscombe
TORQUAY
TOR BAY
Berry Pomeroy
Berry Pomeroy
Blagdon
Totnes
True Street
Collaton St. Mary
PAIGNTON
Guildhall
Longcombe
A385
Higher Yalberton
Goodrington
Goodrington Sands
(Seasonal)
Bowden House
Aish
Goodrington
Sugar Loaf Hill & Saltern Cove
Sharpham
Stoke Gabriel
Elberry Cove
Churston Cove
Berry Head
BERRY HEAD
Ashprington
Bow Creek
Waddeton
Galmpton
Churston Ferrers
Brixham
St. Mary's Bay
Sharkham Point
Cornworthy
East Cornworthy
Dittisham
Paignton & Dartmouth Steam Railway
Prehistoric Hill Settlement
Greenway
Allaleigh
Capton
Hillhead
Man Sands
Long Sands
DARTMOUTH
Kingston
Hillfield
Norton
A3122
Kingswear
Coleton Fishacre
Scabbacombe Head
Kingswear Castle
Ivy Cove
Pudcombe Cove
Millcombe
Fast Rabbit Farm
Dartmouth
Inner Froward Point
Combe Point
Bowden
Burlestone
Blackpool
Stoke Fleming
Leonard's Cove
Blackpool
Matthew's Point
Merrifield
Strete
Forest Cove
Pilchard Cove
Strete Gate
Slapton
Normandy Landings Obelisk
START BAY
Slapton Ley
Stokenham
Sherman Tank
Torcross
Beeson
Beesands
Tinsey Head
Hallsands
Start Point Lighthouse
Nestley Point
START POINT

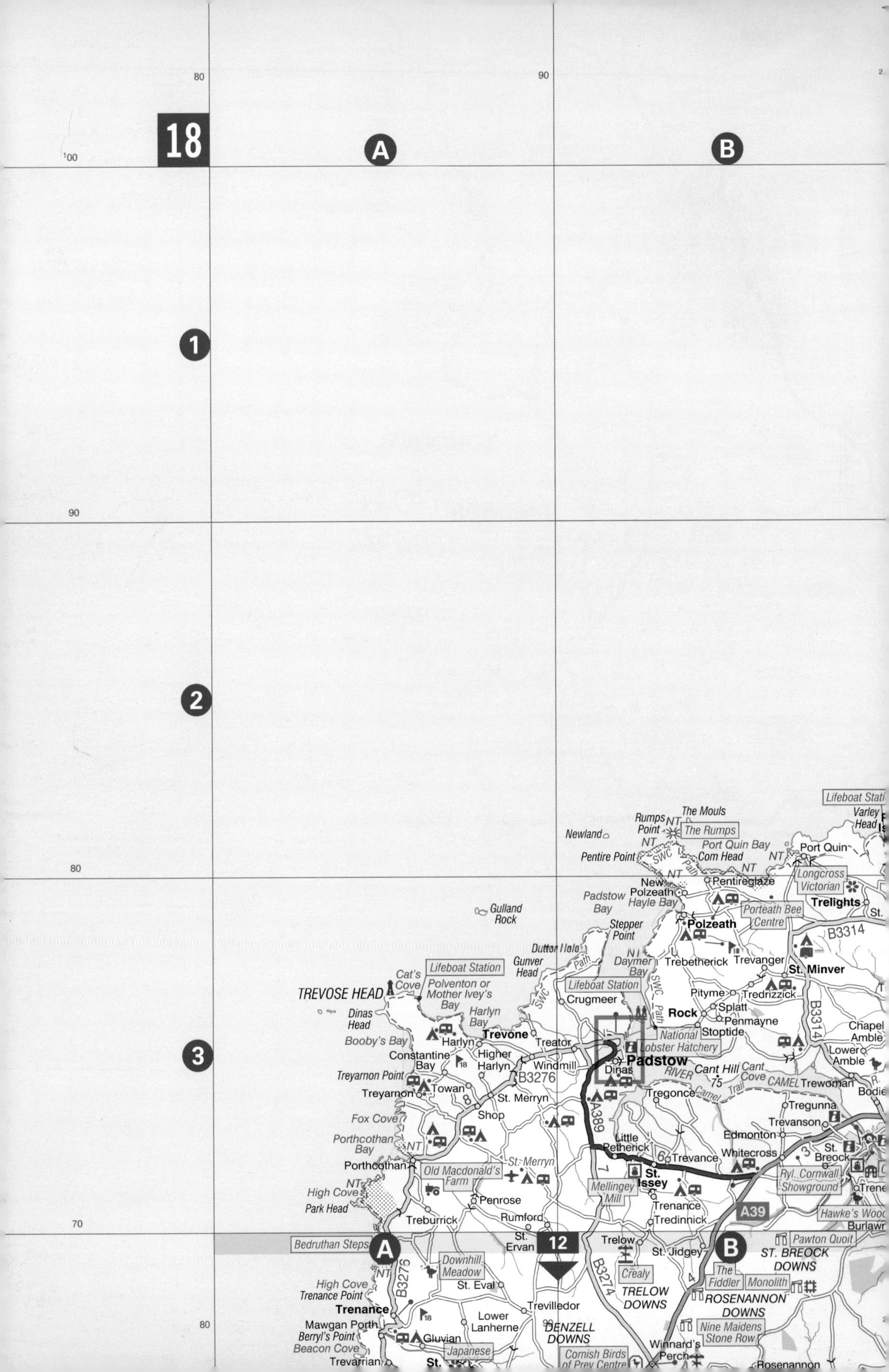

18
A
B
1
2
3
The Mouls
Rumps Point
The Rumps
Newland
Pentire Point
Port Quin Bay
Com Head
Port Quin
Varley Head
Lifeboat Stati
Pentireglaze
Longcross Victorian
New Polzeath
Padstow Bay
Hayle Bay
Trelights
Porteath Bee Centre
Polzeath
Gulland Rock
Stepper Point
B3314
Dutton Hole
Gunver Head
Daymer Bay
Trebetherick
Trevanger
St. Minver
Lifeboat Station
Cat's Cove
Polventon or Mother Ivey's Bay
Lifeboat Station
Crugmeer
Pityme
Tredrizzick
TREVOSE HEAD
Dinas Head
Harlyn Bay
Splatt
Rock
Penmayne
Stoptide
Chapel Amble
Booby's Bay
Harlyn
Trevone
Treator
National Lobster Hatchery
Lower Amble
Constantine Bay
Higher Harlyn
Windmill
Padstow
Dinas
Cant Hill
Cant Cove
RIVER CAMEL
Camel Trail
Trewornan
Treyarnon Point
B3276
Towan
Treyarnon
St. Merryn
Tregonce
Tregunna
Fox Cove
Shop
A389
Trevanson
Porthcothan Bay
Little Petherick
Edmonton
Whitecross
St. Breock
Porthcothan
Old Macdonald's Farm
St. Merryn
Trevance
St. Issey
Ryl. Cornwall Showground
High Cove
Mellingey Mill
Park Head
Penrose
Trenance
Tredinnick
A39
Hawke's Wood
Treburrick
Rumford
Bedruthan Steps
St. Ervan
12
Trelow
St. Jidgey
Pawton Quoit
ST. BREOCK DOWNS
Downhill Meadow
Crealy
The Fiddler
Monolith
High Cove
St. Eval
TRELOW DOWNS
ROSENANNON DOWNS
Tenance Point
B3276
B3274
Trenance
Trevilledor
Lower Lanherne
DENZELL DOWNS
Mawgan Porth
Nine Maidens Stone Row
Berryl's Point
Gluvian
Winnard's Perch
Beacon Cove
Japanese
Cornish Birds of Prey Centre
Trevarrian
Rosenannon

Marhamchurch
Widemouth Bay
Box's Shop
19
Millook Haven
Boscastle
Tintagel
Delabole
Camelford
Davidstow
Hallworthy
Altarnun
St.Teath
St.Tudy
St.Breward
Blisland
Wadebridge
Helland
Cardinham
St.Neot
St.Cleer
Bolventor
BODMIN MOOR
DAVIDSTOW MOOR
Week St.Mary
Warbstow
Jacobstow
Crackington Haven
St.Gennys
A39
A395
A30
A389
B3263
B3266
B3314
B3262
20
13
C
D
1
2
3

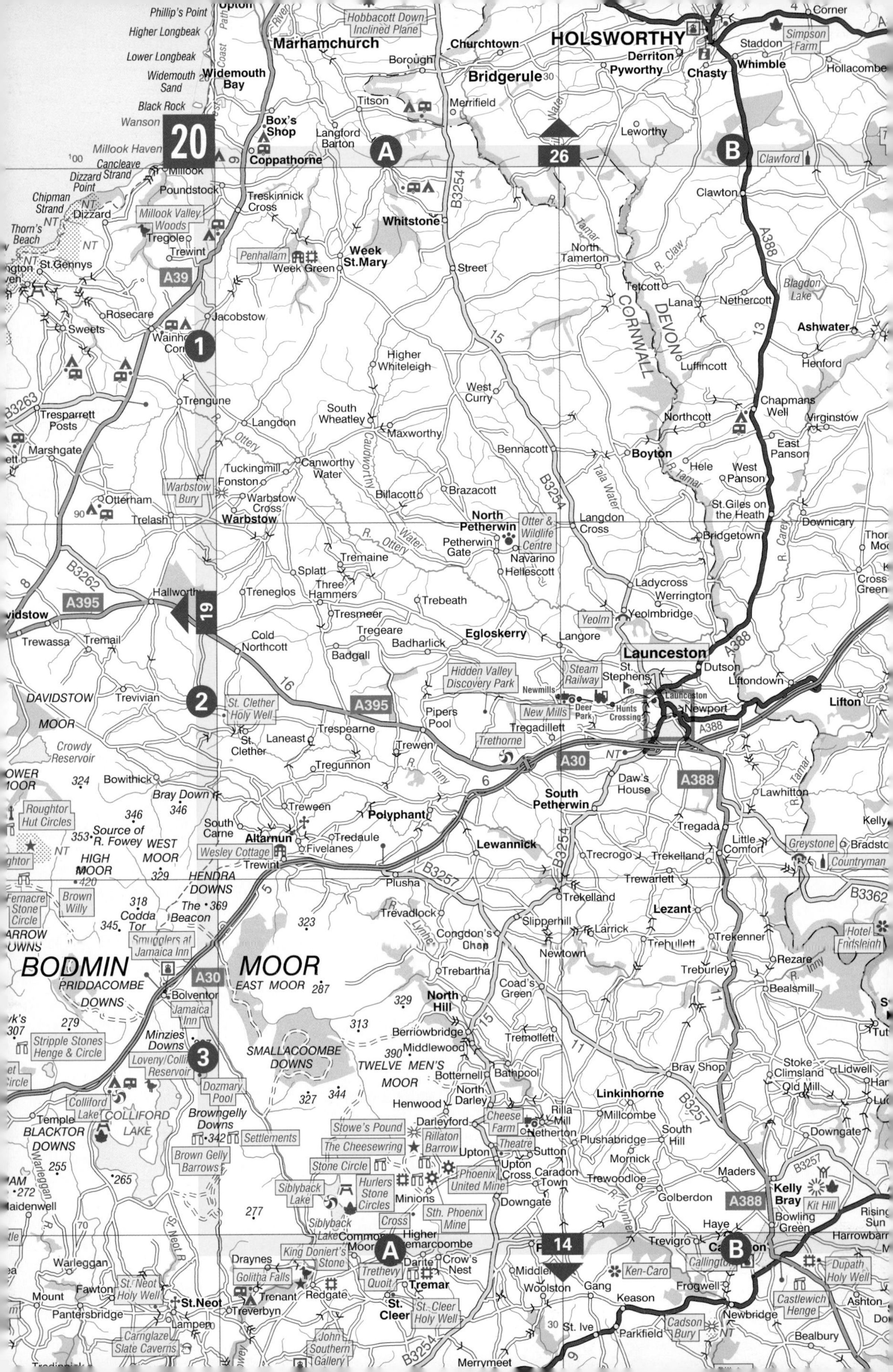

20
26
19
14
HOLSWORTHY
Launceston
BODMIN
MOOR
Marhamchurch
Churchtown
Bridgerule
Derriton
Pyworthy
Chasty
Whimble
Staddon
Simpson Farm
Hollacombe
Corner
Hobbacott Down Inclined Plane
Borough
Titson
Merrifield
Leworthy
Phillip's Point
Higher Longbeak
Lower Longbeak
Widemouth Sand
Widemouth Bay
Black Rock
Wanson
Millook Haven
Box's Shop
Coppathorne
Langford Barton
Clawford
Cancleave Strand
Millook
Dizzard Point
Chipman Strand
Dizzard
Poundstock
Treskinnick Cross
Whitstone
Clawton
Millook Valley Woods
Tregole
Trewint
Thorn's Beach
St.Gennys
Penhallam
Week Green
Week St.Mary
Street
North Tamerton
Tetcott
Lana
Nethercott
Blagdon Lake
Ashwater
Henford
Rosecare
Jacobstow
Sweets
Wainhouse Corner
CORNWALL
DEVON
Luffincott
Higher Whiteleigh
West Curry
South Wheatley
Maxworthy
Chapmans Well
Northcott
Virginstow
Trengune
Langdon
Trespparrett Posts
Marshgate
Bennacott
Boyton
East Panson
Hele
West Panson
Tuckingmill
Fonston
Canworthy Water
Warbstow Bury
Warbstow Cross
Otterham
Billacott
Brazacott
St.Giles on the Heath
Downicary
Trelash
Warbstow
North Petherwin
Otter & Wildlife Centre
Langdon Cross
Petherwin Gate
Navarino
Hellescott
Bridgetown
Tremaine
Splatt
Three Hammers
Treneglos
Hallworthy
Ladycross
Werrington
Davidstow
Trewassa
Tremail
Tresmeer
Trebeath
Yeolm
Yeolmbridge
Cold Northcott
Tregeare
Badharlick
Egloskerry
Langore
Badgall
Dutson
Liftondown
Lifton
St. Stephens
Hidden Valley Discovery Park
Steam Railway
Newmills
Deer Park
Hunts Crossing
Newport
DAVIDSTOW MOOR
Trevivian
St. Clether Holy Well
St. Clether
Pipers Pool
New Mills
Tregadillett
Trespearne
Laneast
Crowdy Reservoir
Trewen
Trethorne
Tregunnon
Daw's House
South Petherwin
Lawhitton
Bowithick
Bray Down
Roughtor Hut Circles
Treween
Polyphant
South Carne
Altarnun
Tredaule
Fivelanes
Lewannick
Tregada
Little Comfort
Greystone
Bradstone
Source of R. Fowey
WEST MOOR
HIGH MOOR
Wesley Cottage
Trewint
Trecrogo
Trekelland
Countryman
HENDRA DOWNS
Plusha
Trewarlett
Fernacre Stone Circle
Brown Willy
Codda Tor
The Beacon
Trevadlock
Lezant
Smugglers at Jamaica Inn
Congdon's Shop
Slipperhill
Larrick
Trebullett
Trekenner
Hotel Endsleigh
Newtown
Treburley
Rezare
PRIDDACOMBE DOWNS
EAST MOOR
Trebartha
Coad's Green
Bealsmill
Bolventor
Jamaica Inn
North Hill
Minzies Downs
Stripple Stones Henge & Circle
Berriowbridge
Middlewood
Tremollett
Loveny/Colliford Reservoir
SMALLACOOMBE DOWNS
TWELVE MEN'S MOOR
Stoke Climsland
Lidwell
Botternell
Bathpool
Bray Shop
Old Mill
Dozmary Pool
Colliford Lake
COLLIFORD LAKE
Temple
BLACKTOR DOWNS
Browngelly Downs
Settlements
Henwood
North Darley
Linkinhorne
Millcombe
Darleyford
Cheese Farm
Rilla Mill
Netherton
Stowe's Pound
Rillaton Barrow
The Cheesewring
South Hill
Plushabridge
Downgate
Brown Gelly Barrows
Upton
Sutton
Theatre
Upton Cross
Caradon Town
Mornick
Stone Circle
Phoenix United Mine
Trewoodloe
Maders
Kelly Bray
Siblyback Lake
Hurlers Stone Circles
Minions
Golberdon
Downgate
Kit Hill
Sth. Phoenix Mine
Siblyback Lake
Cross
Common Moor
Higher Tremarcoombe
Crow's Nest
Trevigro
Haye
Callington
Bowling Green
Harrowbarrow
Draynes
King Doniert's Stone
Darite
Middle
Ken-Caro
Warleggan
Golitha Falls
Trethevy Quoit
Tremar
Woolston
Gang
Frogwell
Dupath Holy Well
Fawton
St. Neot Holy Well
Mount
St.Neot
Trenant
Redgate
St. Cleer
St. Cleer Holy Well
Keason
Newbridge
Castlewich Henge
Ashton
Pantersbridge
Lampen
Treverbyn
St. Ive
Parkfield
Cadson Bury
Carnglaze Slate Caverns
John Southern Gallery
Bealbury
Merrymeet
A39
A395
A30
A388
B3254
B3257
B3262
B3263
B3362
R. Tamar
R. Claw
R. Ottery
R. Inny
R. Lynher
Caudworthy Water
Tala Water

Highampton
Hatherleigh
Brandis Corner
A3079
A3072
Hannaborough
Puworthy Brook
Wagaford Water
Chilla
Lake
Cookworthy
B3216
Jacobstowe
River Okement
Honeychurch
Exbourne
Sampford Courtenay
Week
21
C
D
27
Halwill
Halwill Junction
Beaworthy
Crowden
Northlew
Inwardleigh
West Kimber
East Kimber
Patchacott
Oak Cross
Abbeyford Woods
B3217
Belstone Corner
Rowden
Stowford
Ashbury
Bogtown
Folly Gate
Padson
Brightley
Wadland Barton
Cruft
A386
B3215
Chichacott
Taw Green
Dartmoor Life
Okehampton
B3260
Grindhill
Eworthy
Germansweek
Maddaford
Station
A30
South Tawton
Finch Foundry
Sticklepath
Boasley Cross
Thorndon Cross
Okehampton Camp
Belstone
Ramsley
Bratton Clovelly
ROADFORD LAKE (Reservoir)
Dartmoor
DANGER AREA
Meldon
Meldon Viaduct & Quarry
Thrushel
South Tawton Common
R. Taw
Okehampton Common
Meldon Reservoir
Yes Tor
Roadford Lake
Sourton
Black-a-Tor Copse
Broadwoodwidger
Bridestowe
621
High Willhays
W. Okement R.
Rexon
R. Thrusel
Bidlake
Southerly
Thrushelton
Combebow
Kitty Tor 585
Brim Brook
22
Scorhill Stone Circle
531 Wild Tor
Walla Brook
Berrydown
Stowford
Lewdown
Lobhillcross
R. Lew
Watergate
Shortacombe
586 Great Links Tor
Hangingstone Hill
604
Portgate
Lewtrenchard
460 Brat Tor
541 Chat Tor
Cranmere Pool
601 Whitehorse Hill
Shovel Down Stone Rows
N. Teign R.
Lydford
Dippertown
Eastcott
Lowertown
Devil's Cauldron
Beardon
531 Hare Tor
White Lady Waterfall
NT
Lydford Gorge
Coryton
R. Lyd
Fernworthy Forest Stone Circle
Tavy Cleave
R. Tavy
572 Fur Tor
604 Cut Hill
Marystow
Grey Wethers Stone Circles
North Brentor
Chillaton
Wheal Betsy Engine House
Willsworthy
DARTMOOR
517 Lynch Tor
Brentor
Horndon
Wapsworthy
DARTMOOR NATIONAL PARK
Merripit Hill 449
Mary Tavy
Postbridge
Cudlipptown
465 White Tor
501 Cocks Hill
Lower Godsworthy
Higher Godsworthy
Chaddlehanger
Peter Tavy
Cowsic R.
Powdermills Pottery
B3212
Bellever Forest
492 Black Dunghill
539 Great Mis Tor
Lamerton
Rushford
Portington
Wilminstone
R. Walkham
Wistman's Wood
Clapper
Great Staple Tor
Crockern Tor
Tavistock
Merrivale
Rundlestone
Two Bridges
Millhill
B3357
Vixen Tor
Merrivale Settlement
Dartmoor Prison
Three Oaks
Abbey
TAVISTOCK
Moorshop
Moortown
Princetown
B3362
Latchley
Whitchurch
New Bridge
A390
High Moorland
Tor Royal
Royal Hill 407
R. Tamar
Chilsworthy
Brook
Middlemoor
Sampford Spiney
Strane R.
R. Swincombe
Hexworthy
West Dart R.
Gunnislake
St. Ann's Chapel
Grenofen
Copper
Drakewalls
B3257
R. Lumburn
Whiteworks
Albaston
Morwellham Quay
Horrabridge
Tamar Valley
Norris Green
15
Walkhampton
Burrator Reservoir
471 Crane Hill
Naker's Hill
Cotehele
Calstock
Buckland Monachorum
Garden House
Harrowbeer
Dousland
Quay
Tuckermarsh
Crapstone
Axtown
Yelverton
Sheepstor
Letterbox
Mill
Bohetherick
Bere Alston
Buckland Abbey
Meavy
Upper Plym Valley
Stall Moor Stone Row
Red Lake
Ringmoor Down

Hatherleigh
Lowton
Zeal Monachorum
Down St. Mary
Copplestone
Elston
Honeychurch
North Tawton
Burston
Exbourne
Jacobstowe
Sampford Courtenay
Week
Bow
Knowle
22
Sampford Chapple
Treco
A
28
Nymet Tracey
B
Penstone
Colebrooke
Inwardleigh
Oak Cross
Abbeyford Woods
Belstone Corner
Rowden
Itton
Yeoford
Folly Gate
Padson
Brightley
Hillerton
North Down
Cullaford
Heath Cross
Newbury
Taw Green
Chichacott
Spreyton
Woodland Head
A386
Dartmoor Life
Okehampton
Hittisleigh Barton
Hittisleigh
South Tawton
Finch Foundry
Sticklepath
South Zeal
Belstone
Ramsley
Okehampton
Camp
Dartmoor
Meldon
Meldon Viaduct & Quarry
DANGER AREA
Cheriton Bishop
Cheriton Cross
Whiddon Down
Crockernwell
Gooseford
East Week
South Tawton Common
Okehampton Common
Meldon Reservoir
Throwleigh
Venton
Stone Lane
Drewsteignton
Woodbrooke
Castle Drogo
Prestonbury Castle
Yes Tor
Black-a-Tor Copse
Spinster's Rock
Sandy Park
Fingle
Wonson
Teign Gorge
High Willhays
Murchington
Easton
Cranbrook Castle
Dunsford Woods
Gidleigh
Berrydown
Scorhill Stone Circle
Kitty Tor
Wild Tor
Chagford
Blackaton Wood
Teigncombe
Hangingstone Hill
Great Links Tor
Kestor Settlement
Doccombe
Middlecott
Sloncombe
Moretonhampstead
Chat Tor
Cranmere Pool
Whitehorse Hill
Shovel Down Stone Rows
Frenchbeer
Corndon
Miniature Pony Cen.
Blackingstone Rock
Hare Tor
Fernworthy Reservoir
Fernworthy Forest Stone Circle
Jurston
Hurston
Lettaford
North Bovey
Tavy Cleave
Fur Tor
Cut Hill
Fernworthy Forest
Chagford Common
Grey Wethers Stone Circles
Bennett's Cross
Shapley Tor
Lustleigh Cleave
DANGER AREA
DARTMOOR
DARTMOOR NATIONAL PARK
Lynch Tor
Wapsworthy
Merripit Hill
Vitifer Tin
Heathercombe
Grimspound
Manaton
Water
Lustleigh
Wreyland
Becky Falls Woodland Park
Bowerman's Nose
White Tor
Cocks Hill
Postbridge
Clapper
Barrows
Hamel Down
Hound Tor
Becky Falls
Hound Tor Medieval Village
Granite Tramway
East Dartmoor
Black Dunghill
Powdermills Pottery
Bellever Forest
Bellever
Church House
Bonehill
Haytor Rocks
Haytor Down
House of Teign Valley
Great Mis Tor
Wistman's Wood
Clapper
Widecombe in the Moor
Haytor Vale
Lewthorn Cross
Ilsington
Crockern Tor
Merrivale
Rundlestone
Two Bridges
Shallowford
Dunstone
Foales Arrishes Settlement
Rippon Tor
Merrivale Settlement
Dartmoor Prison
Princetown
Dartmoor Prison
Corndon Tor
Ponsworthy
Blackadon
Buckland in the Moor
Sigford
High Moorland
Tor Royal
Royal Hill
Dartmeet
Dartmeet
Huccaby
Lower Town
Hexworthy
Poundsgate
Ten Commandments Stone
Dart Valley
Caton
Goodstone
Whiteworks
Venford Reservoir
St. Lawrence Chapel
A38
HOLNE MOOR
Hele
Tree
Ashburton
16
Holne
River Dart Adventures
Burrator Reservoir
Crane Hill
Naker's Hill
Michelcombe
Hembury Castle
Forder Green
Dousland
Burrator Reservoir
Scorriton
BUCKFASTLEIGH MOOR
Sheepstor
Letterbox
Abbey
Buckfast
Thornecroft
Stall Moor Stone Row
Red Lake
Clapper
The Valiant Soldier
Railway
Landscove
Upper Plym Valley
DEAN
Buckfastleigh

Chilton
Stockleigh Pomeroy
Chitterley
Livingshayes
Bradninch
Westcott
West Sandford
Upton Hellions
Uppincott
Silverton
Up Exe
Stockwell
Hele
Langford
Plymtree
Sandford
Thorverton
Ellerhayes
Clyst Hydon
CREDITON
A3072
Shobrooke
A396
B3181
23
29
Nether Exe
Killerton
Budlake
Aunk
Devonshire Traditional Breed Centre
Budlake Old Post Office
Rewe
Clyst St. Lawrence
Fordton
Crediton
Sweetham
Smallbrook
Newton St.Cyres
Brampford Speke
Westwood
Uton
Hookway
Ashclyst Forest
Knowle Cross
Stoke Canon
M5
Langford
Huxham
Marker's Cottage
Venny Tedburn
West Town
Half Moon Village
Upton Pyne
Poltimore
Clyston Mill
Broadclyst
Whimple
Oldridge
A377
Cowley
Dog Village
Hand and Pen
Jack-in-the-Green
Stoke Woods
Strete Ralegh
Tedburn St.Mary
Bill Douglas Centre
EXETER
Pinhoe
Rockbeare
Clyst Honiton
EXETER INTERNATIONAL
Allercombe
Pathfinder Village
Whitestone
Whipton
St.James Park
St.David's
Central
A30
Marsh Green
B3212
Polsloe Bridge
Heavitree
Sowton
Halstow
Wheatley
Bowhill
St. Thomas
EXETER
Aylesbeare
Digby & Sowton
Devon County Showground
Longdown
A3015
Farringdon
B3184
Perkin's Village
B3180
Farringdon Cross
Clyst St.Mary
Culver
Ide
A379
A3052
White Cross
Nine Oaks
Reedy
Alphington
River Exe
Countess Wear
Crealy Great Adventure Park
Steps Bridge
B3193
Shillingford Abbot
Old Sludge Beds
Exe Reed Beds
Topsham
Clyst St.George
Woodbury Salterton
Hawkerland
Shillingford St.George
Topsham
Dunchideock
Exminster
Ebford
Woodbury Castle
Webberton Cross
Clapham
Brenton
Topsham
A376
24
Woodbury
B3179
Stowford
Bridford
Bridfordmills
Doddiscombsleigh
Haldon Belvedere (Lawrence Castle)
Kennford
Exton
Exton
Exminster Marshes
Lympstone Commando
Bird of Prey
Kenn
Woodmanton
Yettington
Higher Ashton
Kennick Resr.
Christow
Bennah
Bullers Hill
Powderham
Lympstone
Lympstone Village
Lower Ashton
Powderham
Tottiford Resr.
A380
Kenton
A La Ronde
Bystock
Hulham
A38
Devon & Exeter
R. Exe
Withycombe Raleigh
Canonteign Falls
Trusham
Starcross
Starcross
Exmouth
EXMOUTH
Littleham
Harcombe
Mamhead
Exmouth
Hennock
Teign Village
(Seasonal)
World of Country Life
Hazelwood
B3193
Great 00 Model Rlwy.
Cockwood
Exe Estuary
Otter Cove
Town Mills
Waddon
Ashcombe
Lifeboat Station
Dawlish Warren
Sandy Bay
Straight Point
Chudleigh
Bovey Tracey
Devon Guild of Craftsmen
B3344
Rock
Ugbrooke Park
Dawlish Warren
Langstone Rock
Chudleigh Knighton
Heritage Centre
Bovey Heath
Gappah
Ideford
Dawlish Water
Teapottery
Luton
Heathfield
B3192
Dawlish
Dawlish
Dawlish
Coryton's Cove
Horse Cove
Humber
Coldeast
Stover
Preston
Holcombe
Trago Mills
Teigngrace
A382
Orchid Paradise
Rural Life
Sprey Point
Kingsteignton
Bishopsteignton
Teignmouth
Gorse Blossom
Teignmouth & Shaldon
South Knighton
Mile End
A381
RIVER TEIGN
Shaldon
Highweek
Hackney Marshes
Ringmore
Grand Pier
A383
Newton Abbot
Lifeboat Station
NEWTON ABBOT
Combeinteignhead
Wildlife Trust
Netherton
Labrador Bay
West Ogwell
Bradley
Plant World
Stokeinteignhead
East Ogwell
Wolborough
A380
17
Lower Gabwell
Prickly Ball Farm (Hedgehog Hospital)
Decoy
Higher Gabwell
Abbotskerswell
BABBACOMBE
Denbury
Pleasant View Nursery
Coffinswell
Maidencombe
Daccombe
BAY
Two Mile Oak
Kingskerswell
Watcombe Head
Ipplepen
Torbryan
Dainton
North Whilborough
Combe Pafford
Model Village

24
30
23
A
B
1
2
3
EXETER
EXMOUTH
SIDMOUTH
Honiton
Ottery St. Mary
Budleigh Salterton
Dawlish
Teignmouth
Bradninch
Silverton
Livingshayes
Stockwell
Hele
Ellerhayes
Westcott
Norman's Green
Colliton
Clyst William
Plymtree
Langford
Luton
Upton
Godford Cross
Combe Raleigh
Awliscombe
Payhembury
Clyst Hydon
Lower Tale
Higher Tale
Lower Cheriton
Higher Cheriton
Colestocks
Buckerell
Weston
Hembury
Killerton
Budlake
Old Post Office
Clyst St. Lawrence
Westwood
Talaton
Newtown
Feniton
Fenny Bridges
Hamlet
Allhallows
Offwell
Ashclyst Forest
Stoke Canon
Huxham
Poltimore
Marker's Cottage
Broadclyst
Clyston Mill
Knowle Cross
Whimple
Larkbeare
Escot Park
Gittisham
Alfington
Taleford
Woodford
Fairmile
Coombelake
Cadhay
Tumbling Weir
Church Green
Farway Hill Barrows
Farway
Farway Countryside Park
Dog Village
Jack-in-the-Green
Hand and Pen
Strete Ralegh
Rockbeare
Pinhoe
Whipton
Clyst Honiton
Exeter International
Allercombe
Marsh Green
West Hill
Broad Oak
Fluxton
Wiggaton
Ark Pottery
East Hill
Broad Down
Blackbury Camp
Sand
Cotford
Sidbury
Heavitree
Sowton
Digby & Sowton
Devon County Showground
Aylesbeare
Metcombe
Coombe
Tipton St. John
Venn Ottery
Farringdon
Perkin's Village
Southerton
Clyst St.Mary
Farringdon Cross
White Cross
Nine Oaks
Aylesbeare Common
Harpford
Bowd
Stowford
Sidford
Harcombe
The Donkey Sanctuary
Bulstone
Countess Wear
Exe Reed Beds
Crealy Great Adventure Park
Clyst St.George
Woodbury Salterton
Burrow
Goosemoor
Newton Poppleford
Northmostown
Bulverton
Sid
Observatory
Salcombe Regis
Weston
Street
Topsham
Exminster
Ebford
Hawkerland
Stoneyford
Kingston
Woodbury Castle
Woodbury
Colaton Raleigh
Cotmaton
Salcombe Mouth
Weston Mouth
Littlecombe
Exton
Exminster Marshes
Lympstone Commando
Stowford
Bicton College
Bicton Park
Bicton Woodland
Countryside
Sid Vale Heritage Centre
Woodmanton
Yettington
North Star
Otterton
Mill
Ladram Bay
Chiselbury Bay
Crab Ledge
Brandy Head
Black Head
Powderham
Lympstone
Lympstone Village
East Budleigh
Kenton
A La Ronde
Bystock
Hulham
Withycombe Raleigh
Knowle
Otter Estuary
Starcross
Exmouth
(Seasonal)
Littleham
World of Country Life
Fairlynch
Great 00 Model Rlwy.
Cockwood
Exe Estuary
Lifeboat Station
Littleham Cove
Otter Cove
Dawlish Warren
Sandy Bay
Straight Point
Langstone Rock
Coryton's Cove
Horse Cove
Holcombe
Sprey Point
Teignmouth & Shaldon
Grand Pier
Lifeboat Station
Wildlife Trust
Labrador Bay
BABBACOMBE BAY
M5
A30
A35
A373
A375
A3052
A379
A376
B3181
B3174
B3177
B3180
B3184
B3179
B3178
B3176
NT
SWC
Path
R. Culm
R. Clyst
R. Exe
R. Otter
R. Sid
River Tale
Exeter Canal
70
80
90
300
10

Chardstock
Axminster
Kilmington
Musbury
Colyton
Colyford
Axmouth
Seaton
Beer
Uplyme
LYME REGIS
Charmouth
Morcombelake
Chideock
Bridport
Hawkchurch
Wilmington
Broadwindsor
Stoke Abbott
LYME BAY
SEATON BAY
Golden Cap
Golden Cap Cliffs
Dinosaurland
Lyme Regis
Axmouth-Lyme Undercliffs
Pecorama at Beer
Axe Valley Heritage
Beer Quarry
Tramway
Shute Barton
Loughwood Meeting Ho.
Forde Abbey
Membury Castle
Lambert's Castle
Coney's Castle
Marshwood Castle
Pilsden Pen
Trinity Hill
Uplyme Pinetum
Black Ven & The Spittles
Town Mill
Lifeboat Station
Craft & Design Centre
A35
A358
A3052
B3165
B3162
B3164
B3174
B3172
B3261
31
25
C
D
1
2
3
30
40
70
80
90

26
A
32
B
20
30
BARNSTAPLE
BIDEFORD
Barley Bay
Shipload Bay
Chapman Rock
Beckland Bay
HARTLAND POINT
NT
South West Coast Path
NT Windbury Point
Blackchurch Rock
Titchberry
Exmansworthy
Damehole Point
Hartland Abbey
Abbey River
Norton
NT
Wood Rock
Gallant Rock
Clovelly
Bight a Doubleyou
Babbacombe Mouth
Babbacombe Cliff
Higher Rowden
Cornborough
Hartland Quay
Hartland Quay
Stoke
Hartland
Velly
B3237
Fisherman's Cottage
Buck's & Keivell's Woods
Gauter Point
St. Catherine's Tor
Hartland Pottery
Rosedown
Higher Clovelly
Speke's Mill Mouth
Speke's Mill Mouth Waterfall
Natcott
B3248
Clovelly Dykes
Kingsley
Hobby Drive
Buck's Mills
Horns Cross
Longpeak
Milford
Docton Mill
A39
Waytown
Philham
The Milky Way Adventure Park
Buck's Cross
River Yeo
Elmscott
Edistone
Welsford
West Town
Cranford
Parkham
Clifford Water
Woolfardisworthy or Woolsery
Parkham Ash
Gull Rock
South Hole
Alminstone Cross
Embury Beach
Lutsford
Huddisford
Melbury Resr.
Knaps Longpeak
Welcombe
Lower Twitchen
Welcombe Mouth
Darracott
Ashmansworthy
Mead
Meddon
Marsland Mouth
Marsland Water
Dipple
Gull Rock
Woolley
East Putford
Yeol Mouth
Gooseham
Eastcott
East Youlstone
Crimp
Lucky Hole
Morwenstow
West Youlstone
Dinworthy
Gnome Reserve
West Putford
River Waldon
River Torridge
Higher Sharpnose Point
Hawker's Hut
Shop
Killarney Springs
Colscott
Haytown
Woodford
Bradworthy
Stanbury Mouth
Lamberal Water
Upper Tamar Lake
Tamar Lakes
Brendon
Abbots Bickington
Lower Sharpnose Point
Brocklands Adventure Park
Steeple Point
Coombe Valley
Kilkhampton
Alfardisworthy
Sutcombe
Coombe
NT
Lower Tamar Lake
Sutcombemill
Shop
Duckpool
Kilkhampton
Thorne
Forda
Thurdon
River Waldon
Venngreen
Stibb
Tamar Lakes
Soldon Cross
Milton Damerel
Sandy Mouth
B3254
River Neet
Long Rock
A39
Woodsdown Hill
Menachurch Point
CORNWALL
DEVON
Dexbeer
Northcott Mouth
Holsworthy Beacon
Woodacott
Maer
Hersham
BUDE
Poughill
Bush
Lana
BAY
Flexbury
1643
Crooklets Beach
Stamford Hill
STRATTON
Grimscott
Small Brook
Thorne Farm
Bude Haven
Chilsworthy
Bude Marshes
A3072
Launcells Cross
Pancrasweek
A388
Lynstone
BUDE
Red Post
A3072
Cookbury Wick
Thorne
Phillip's Point
Upton
Anvil Corner
Hobbacott Down Inclined Plane
Higher Longbeak
HOLSWORTHY
Simpson Farm
Marhamchurch
Churchtown
Staddon
Lower Longbeak
Borough
Derriton
Chasty
Whimble
Hollacombe
Widemouth Sand
Widemouth Bay
Bridgerule
Pyworthy
Black Rock
Titson
Merrifield
Wanson Mouth
Box's Shop
Langford Barton
Leworthy
Millook Haven
Coppathorne
Clawford
Cancleave Strand
Millook
Dizzard Point
Poundstock
Claw
Chipman Strand
Dizzard
Treskinnick Cross
Millook Valley Woods
Whitstone
Thorn's Beach
Tregole
Week St.Mary
North Tamerton
R. Claw
Trewint
Penhallam
St.Gennys
Week Green
Street
Tetcott
Blagdon Lake
Tamar
Deer
River Neet
South West Coast Path

BARNSTAPLE
Braunton Burrows
Bradiford
Pottington
Goodleigh
Gunn
Bradninch
Fremington
Muddlebridge
Sticklepath
Isley Marshes
River Taw
Tarka Trail
Fort Hill
Jungleland
Newport
Stoodleigh
Accott
A361
Yelland
Bickington
Lake
Landkey
Rumsam
Landkey Newland
Northam Burrows
Lifeboat Station
North Devon Maritime
B3233
Worlington
Bickleton
Brynsworthy
Bishop's Tawton
Tordown Farm
27
Riverton
Westward Ho!
Pebble Ridge
Appledore
Instow
Signal Box
33
Tawstock
Eastacombe
Church
St. John's Chapel
Swimbridge
Hannaford
Marshford Organic
Tapeley Park
A39
A377
B3236
A386
River Torridge
Buckleigh
Northam
Westleigh
Holmacott
Silford
Heddon
Filleigh
Horwood
Eastleigh
Orchard Hill
Raleigh Hill
Abbotsham
Burton Art Gallery
Chudleigh Fort
Lower Lovacott
Week
Harracott
Cobbaton
Stowford
East Stowford
East-the-Water
BIDEFORD
Railway
Woodtown
Stony Cross
Newton Tracey
Hiscott
Chapelton
Herner
Langham Lake
Combat Collection
Chittlehampton
Gammaton
Jennetts Resr.
Alverdiscott
Gammaton Resrs.
Atlantis Adventure Park
Ford
A386
Gammaton Moor
B3232
B3227
Landcross
Woodtown
Yarnscombe
Umberleigh
Atherington
Huntshaw Water
Hallspill
Littleham
River Yeo
Cross
Warkleigh
Huntshaw
Saltrens
Weare Giffard
207
Langridgeford
B3217
The Downes
Darracott Resr.
Buckland Brewer
High Bullen
Sherwood Green
High Bickington
Chittlehamholt
Monkleigh
Dartington Crystal
GREAT TORRINGTON
River Duntz
A388
Priory
Stevenstone
Burwood
St. Giles in the Wood
196
Ebberley Hill
Portsmouth Arms
River Taw
Kingford
Frithelstock
Torrington 1646
A377
Taddiport
Frithelstock Stone
Tythecott
B3227
The Plough Arts Centre
North Healand
Kingscott
28
Roborough
Junction Pool
Southcott
RHS Rosemoor
A3124
Little Torrington
Beaford Brook
King's Nympton
Burrington
Aylescott
Mully Brook
Langtree
Withacott
Stibb Cross
Great Potheridge
Beaford
East Westacott
Riddlecombe
Tarka Trail
Berry Cross
Little Potheridge
River Torridge
Ashreigney
Peters Marland
Winswell
Newton St. Petrock
River Mere
Woollaton
A386
Barometer World
Merton
Dolton
Halsdon
Hollacombe Town
East Ashley
Huish
Little Mere River
Caute
Dowland
Hollocombe
Battledown Cross
Buckland Filleigh
North Town
Upcott
Shebbear
Dumpinghill New Inn
Petrockstowe
Winkleigh
Highworthy
Meeth
Iddesleigh
Barwick
Folly Cross
Ingleigh Green
B3220
River Torridge
Cookbury
Holemoor
Sheepwash
Black Torrington
Broadwoodkelly
A3124
Monkokehampton
Obelisk
Hole Brook
Bondleigh
Highampton
Brandis Corner
Hatherleigh
A3072
Hannaborough
Honeychurch
B3216
A3079
Wagaford Water
Pulworthy Brook
Chilla
Lake
Cookworthy
Exbourne
River Okement
Jacobstowe
Sampford Courtenay
Week
Sampford Chapple
A3072
A386
Trecott
Halwill
Halwill Junction
Beaworthy
Crowden
21
Northlew
Inwardleigh
West Kimber
East Kimber
Oak Cross
Abbeyford Woods
Belstone Corner
Rowden
Patchacott
Ashbury
Folly Gate
Sampford Courtenay
Stowford
Bogtown
Padson
Brightley
B3215
A3079
Wadland Barton
Cruft
Chichacott
Taw Green

BARNSTAPLE
Goodleigh
Brayford
High Bray
North Radworthy
Fort Hill
Newport
Landkey
Rumsam
Bishop's Tawton
Swimbridge
Swimbridge Newland
Hannaford
Tawstock
Jungleland
Devon
Church
Gunn
Bradninch
Stoodleigh Barton
Stoodleigh
Accott
Tordown Farm
West Buckland
East Buckland
Charles
Charles Bottom
Popham
North Heasley
Heasley Mill
South Radworthy
Flitton Oak
Millbrook
North Molton
Riverton
Heddon
Castle Hill
Filleigh
Stag's Head
Mornacott
Sheepwash
Aller
River Yeo
Bish Mill
Newtown
Bishop's Nympton
Avercombe
Ash Mill
Quince Honey Farm
South Molton
SOUTH MOLTON
River Mole
Clapworthy
Hancock's Devon Cider
George Nympton
Alswear
Crooked Oak
Mariansleigh
Rose Ash
Romansleigh
Meshaw
Harracott
Week
Chapelton
Herner
Hiscott
Langham Lake
Cobbaton
Stowford
East Stowford
Combat Collection
Chittlehampton
Yarnscombe
Umberleigh
Atherington
Cross
Warkleigh
Satterleigh
Langridgeford
Sherwood Green
High Bickington
Chittlehamholt
River Bray
River Mole
King's Nympton
St. Giles in the Wood
Ebberley Hill
Kingford
Portsmouth Arms
River Taw
Junction Pool
Kingscott
Roborough
Burrington
Aylescott
Mully Brook
Beaford
Beaford Brook
River Torridge
Riddlecombe
East Westacott
Ashreigney
Week
Huntacott Water
Lutworthy
Chulmleigh
Little Dart River
Cheldon
East Worlington
West Worlington
Chawleigh
Thelbridge Barton
Bridge Reeve
Eggesford
Heywood
Eggesford
Country Centre
Hilltown Wood
Eggesford Barton
Dolton
Halsdon
Hollacombe Town
East Ashley
Hollocombe
Filleigh
River Datch
Dowland
Upcott
Wembworthy
Nymet Rowland
Lapford
Eastington
Iddesleigh
Barwick
Winkleigh
Coldridge
Lapford Cross
Morchard Bishop
Ingleigh Green
Brushford
Broadwoodkelly
West Leigh
East Leigh
Weeke
Oldborough
Monkokehampton
Obelisk
Hatherleigh
Bondleigh
River Taw
Lowton
Gissage Lake
Down St. Mary
Morchard Road
Down St. Mary
Zeal Monachorum
Copplestone
Elston
Honeychurch
Exbourne
River Okement
Jacobstowe
North Tawton
Week
Burston
Bow
Knowle
Sampford Courtenay
Sampford Chapple
Trecott
Nymet Tracey
Colebrooke
Penstone
Inwardleigh
Oak Cross
Abbeyford Woods
Belstone Corner
Rowden
Itton
Hillerton
Yeoford
North Down
Folly Gate
Padson
Brightley
Chichacott
Taw Green
Cullaford
Heath Cross
Spreyton
Newbury
R. Troney
28
34
27
22
A
B
A361
A377
A399
A3124
A3072
A386
B3227
B3226
B3137
B3217
B3096
B3042
B3220
B3216
B3215

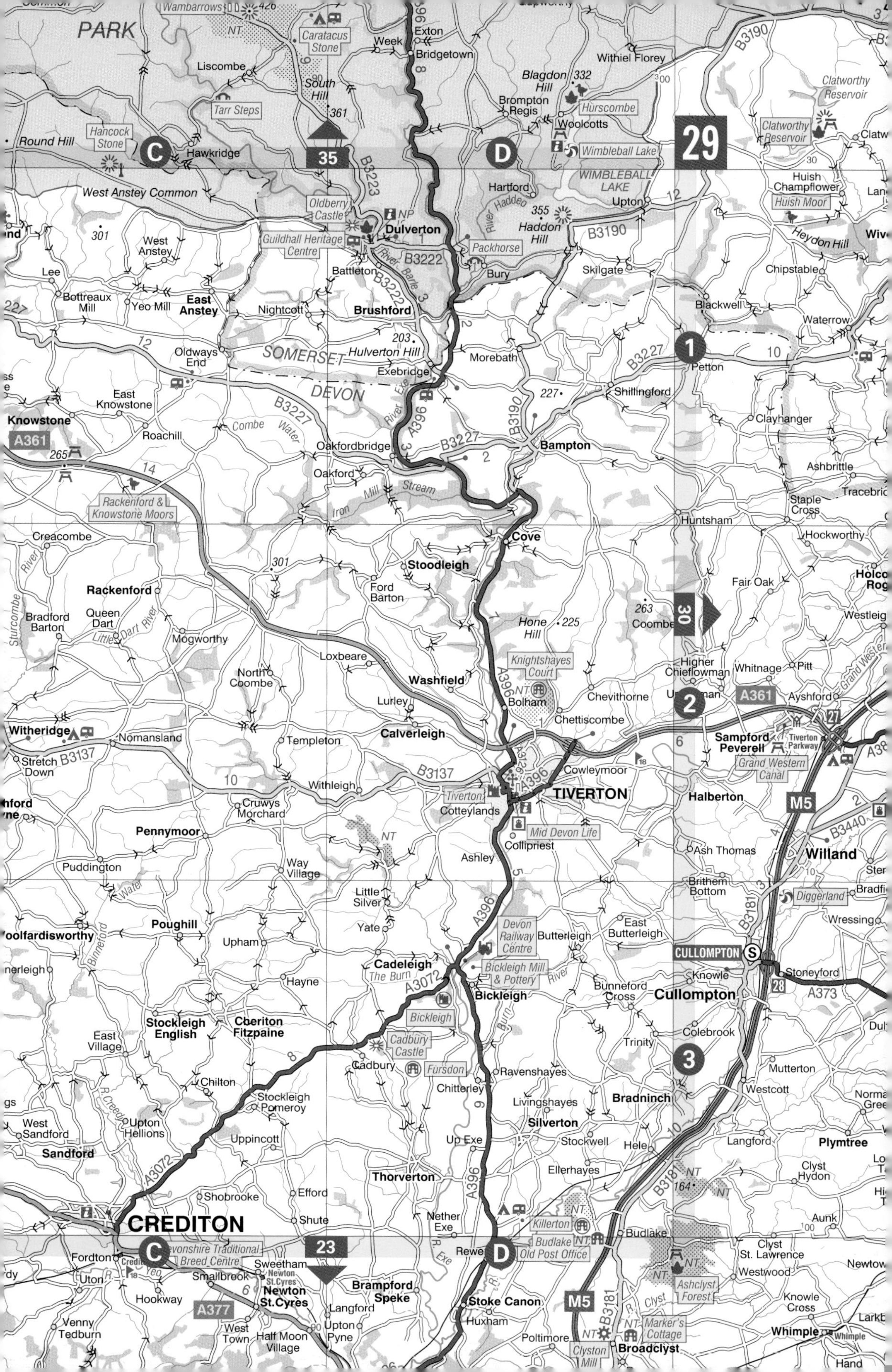

PARK
Wambarrows
426
NT
Caratacus Stone
Exton
Week
Bridgetown
Withiel Florey
B3190
Clatworthy Reservoir
Liscombe
South Hill
361
Blagdon Hill
332
Brompton Regis
Hurscombe
Woolcotts
Tarr Steps
Hancock Stone
Round Hill
Hawkridge
C
35
B3223
D
Wimbleball Lake
WIMBLEBALL LAKE
29
Clatworthy Reservoir
Huish Champflower
Huish Moor
West Anstey Common
Oldberry Castle
Dulverton
Hartford
River Haddeo
355
Haddon Hill
Upton
12
Heydon Hill
301
West Anstey
Guildhall Heritage Centre
B3222
Packhorse
B3190
Lee
Battleton
River Barle
Bury
Skilgate
Chipstable
Bottreaux Mill
Yeo Mill
East Anstey
Nightcott
Brushford
Blackwell
203
Waterrow
Oldways End
SOMERSET
Hulverton Hill
Morebath
B3227
1
Petton
10
Exebridge
DEVON
Shillingford
East Knowstone
227
Knowstone
Roachill
Combe Water
River Exe
A396
B3190
Clayhanger
A361
265
Oakfordbridge
B3227
Bampton
Oakford
Iron Mill Stream
Ashbrittle
14
Rackenford & Knowstone Moors
Staple Cross
Tracebridge
Huntsham
Creacombe
Cove
Hockworthy
301
Stoodleigh
Fair Oak
Rackenford
Ford Barton
263
Coombe
30
Bradford Barton
Queen Dart
Little Dart River
Sturcombe River
Mogworthy
Hone Hill
225
Westleigh
Loxbeare
Knightshayes Court
Higher Chieflowman
Whitnage
Pitt
North Coombe
Washfield
Lurley
Bolham
Chevithorne
2
A361
Ayshford
Grand Western
Witheridge
Nomansland
Calverleigh
Chettiscombe
Templeton
Sampford Peverell
Tiverton Parkway
27
Stretch Down
B3137
Cowleymoor
Grand Western Canal
10
Withleigh
Tiverton
TIVERTON
Halberton
M5
Cruwys Morchard
Cotteylands
Mid Devon Life
B3440
Pennymoor
Colliprest
Ash Thomas
Willand
Puddington
Ashley
Way Village
Brithem Bottom
Little Silver
Diggerland
Poughill
Yate
Butterleigh
East Butterleigh
Wressing
Woolfardisworthy
Upham
Devon Railway Centre
CULLOMPTON
Cadeleigh
Bickleigh Mill & Pottery
The Burn
Knowle
Stoneyford
Hayne
A3072
Bickleigh
Bunneford Cross
Cullompton
28
A373
Stockleigh English
Cheriton Fitzpaine
Colebrook
East Village
Cadbury Castle
Trinity
3
Cadbury
Fursdon
Ravenshayes
Mutterton
Chilton
Chitterley
Westcott
Bradninch
Stockleigh Pomeroy
Livingshayes
West Sandford
Upton Hellions
Silverton
Uppincott
Up Exe
Stockwell
Hele
Langford
Plymtree
Sandford
Ellerhayes
Thorverton
Clyst Hydon
164
Shobrooke
Efford
Aunk
Nether Exe
Killerton
Shute
CREDITON
Budlake Old Post Office
Budlake
23
Rewe
Clyst St. Lawrence
Fordton
Devonshire Traditional Breed Centre
Sweetham
Newton St.Cyres
Westwood
Newtown
Uton
Smallbrook
Brampford Speke
Ashclyst Forest
Hookway
Newton St.Cyres
Stoke Canon
M5
Knowle Cross
A377
Langford
Huxham
Marker's Cottage
Venny Tedburn
West Town
Upton Pyne
Whimple
Half Moon Village
Poltimore
Broadclyst
Clyston Mill

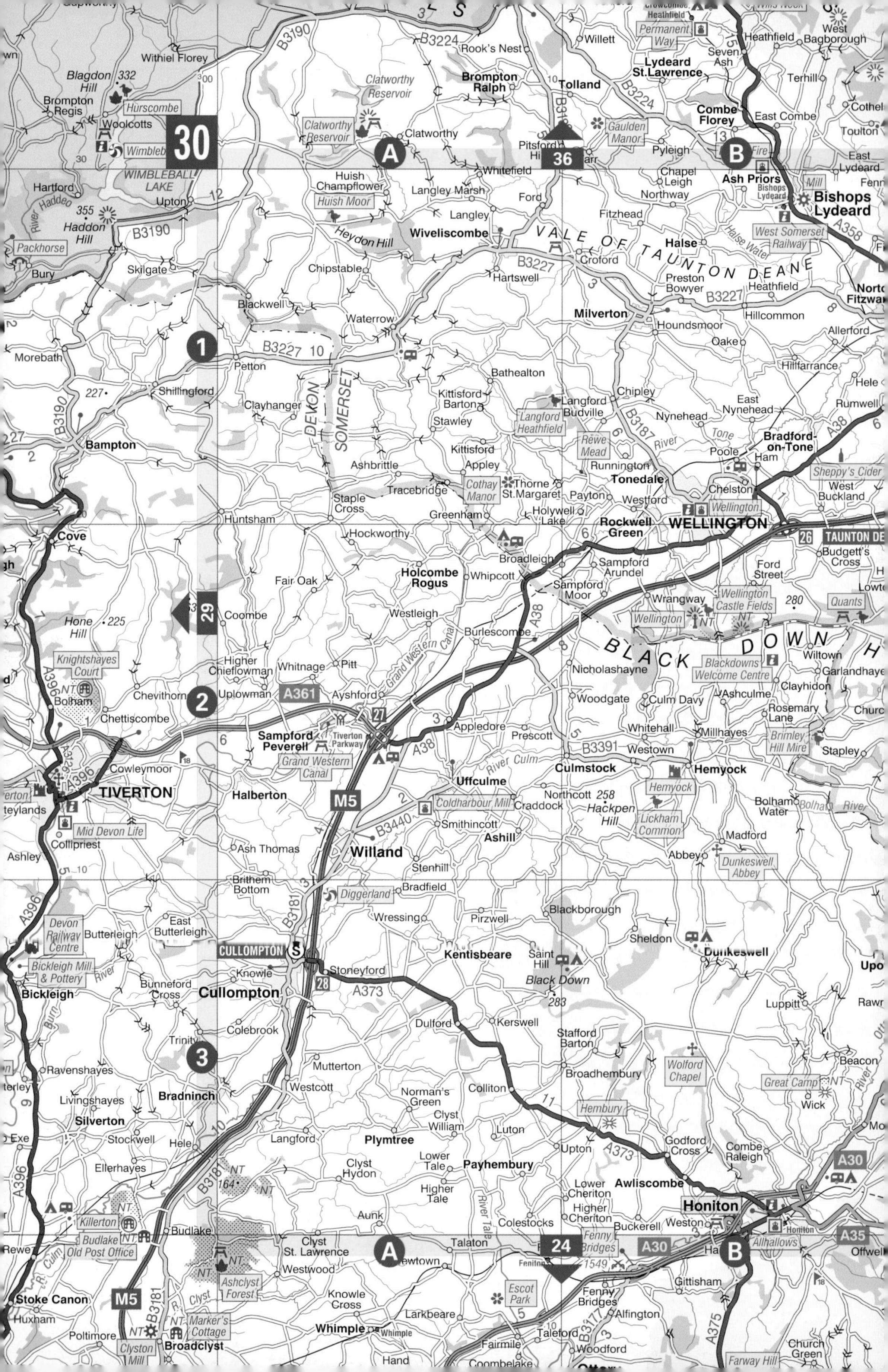

30
36
29
24
26
27
28
A
B
1
2
3
Withiel Florey
Blagdon Hill
332
Brompton Regis
Hurscombe
Woolcotts
Wimbleball
WIMBLEBALL LAKE
Hartford
River Haddeo
Upton
355
Haddon Hill
B3190
Packhorse
Bury
Skilgate
B3224
Rook's Nest
Clatworthy Reservoir
Brompton Ralph
Clatworthy
Huish Champflower
Huish Moor
Whitefield
Langley Marsh
Langley
Heydon Hill
Wiveliscombe
Chipstable
Blackwell
Waterrow
Morebath
B3227
Petton
Shillingford
227
Clayhanger
DEVON
SOMERSET
Bampton
Ashbrittle
Staple Cross
Huntsham
Cove
Hockworthy
Fair Oak
Hone Hill
225
Coombe
Knightshayes Court
NT
Bolham
Chevithorne
Higher Chieflowman
Uplowman
Chettiscombe
Whitnage
Pitt
Ayshford
Grand Western Canal
A361
A396
Cowleymoor
TIVERTON
Sampford Peverell
Tiverton Parkway
Halberton
Mid Devon Life
Collipriest
Ashley
Ash Thomas
Brithem Bottom
M5
Willand
B3181
Devon Railway Centre
Butterleigh
East Butterleigh
Bickleigh Mill & Pottery
Bickleigh
Bunneford Cross
CULLOMPTON
Cullompton
Knowle
Colebrook
Trinity
Ravenshayes
Livingshayes
Bradninch
Silverton
Stockwell
Hele
Exe
Ellerhayes
164
Killerton
Budlake NT Old Post Office
Budlake
Rewe
River Culm
Ashclyst Forest
Stoke Canon
Huxham
Poltimore
Marker's Cottage
Clyston Mill
Broadclyst
Willett
Lydeard St.Lawrence
Tolland
Gaulden Manor
Pitsford Hill
Combe Florey
Pyleigh
Chapel Leigh
Northway
Ford
Fitzhead
VALE OF TAUNTON DEANE
Croford
Hartswell
Milverton
Halse
Preston Bowyer
Heathfield
Hillcommon
Houndsmoor
Oake
Bathealton
Kittisford Barton
Stawley
Kittisford
Appley
Langford Budville
Langford Heathfield
Rewe Mead
Runnington
Cothay Manor
Thorne St.Margaret
Tracebridge
Greenham
Holywell Lake
Payton
Westford
Tonedale
Rockwell Green
WELLINGTON
Broadleigh
Holcombe Rogus
Whipcott
Sampford Arundel
Sampford Moor
Westleigh
Burlescombe
A38
BLACK DOWN HILLS
Nicholashayne
Woodgate
Culm Davy
Appledore
Prescott
Culmstock
B3391
Westown
Whitehall
Millhayes
Hemyock
Uffculme
River Culm
Coldharbour Mill
Craddock
Northcott
258
Hackpen Hill
Lickham Common
B3440
Smithincott
Ashill
Stenhill
Bradfield
Diggerland
Wressing
Pirzwell
Blackborough
Sheldon
Dunkeswell
Kentisbeare
Saint Hill
Black Down
283
Stoneyford
A373
Dulford
Kerswell
Stafford Barton
Broadhembury
Mutterton
Westcott
Norman's Green
Colliton
Clyst William
Hembury
Luton
Langford
Plymtree
Lower Tale
Payhembury
Upton
Clyst Hydon
Higher Tale
River Tale
Lower Cheriton
Higher Cheriton
Awliscombe
Aunk
Colestocks
Buckerell
Clyst St. Lawrence
Talaton
Westwood
Knowle Cross
Larkbeare
Whimple
Escot Park
Fenny Bridges
A30
Gittisham
Alfington
Taleford
Fairmile
Woodford
Coombelake
Hand
B3177
1549
Heathfield
Seven Ash
West Bagborough
Terhill
Cothelstone
East Combe
Toulton
East Lydeard
Ash Priors
Bishops Lydeard
Mill
A358
West Somerset Railway
Halse Water
Norton Fitzwarren
Allerford
Hillfarrance
Hele
East Nynehead
Nynehead
Rumwell
B3187
Tone River
Poole
Bradford-on-Tone
Ham
Chelston
Sheppy's Cider
West Buckland
TAUNTON DEANE
Budgett's Cross
Ford Street
Wrangway
Wellington Castle Fields
Wellington
280
Quants
Wiltown
Blackdowns Welcome Centre
Garlandhayes
Ashculme
Clayhidon
Rosemary Lane
Brimley Hill Mire
Stapley
Bolham Water
Bolham River
Madford
Abbey
Dunkeswell Abbey
Luppitt
Wolford Chapel
Great Camp
Beacon
Wick
Godford Cross
Combe Raleigh
A30
Honiton
Weston
Allhallows
A35
Offwell
A375
Church Green
Farway Hill
Rawridge

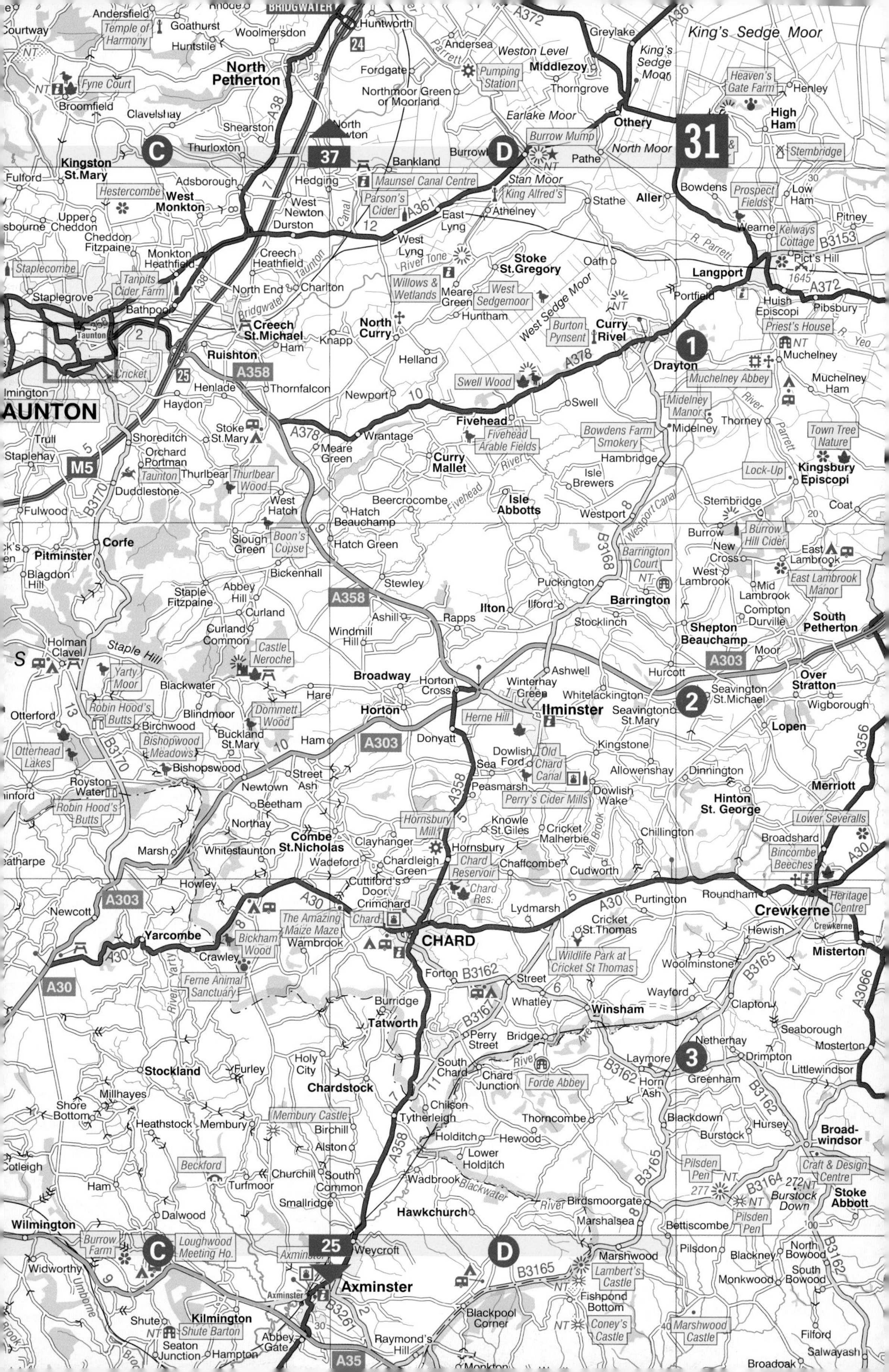
BRIDGWATER
Andersfield
Courtway
Temple of Harmony
Goathurst
Huntstile
Woolmersdon
Huntworth
24
A372
Greylake
A361
King's Sedge Moor
Andersea
Weston Level
King's Sedge Moor
North Petherton
Fordgate
Pumping Station
Middlezoy
Heaven's Gate Farm
Henley
Fyne Court
NT
Northmoor Green or Moorland
Thorngrove
Broomfield
Clavelshay
A38
Earlake Moor
Othery
High Ham
Shearston
North Newton
Burrow Mump
31
C
Thurloxton
37
Bankland
Burrowbridge
D
Pathe
North Moor
Stembridge
Kingston St.Mary
Stan Moor
Fulford
Adsborough
Hedging
Mansel Canal Centre
King Alfred's
Bowdens
Prospect Fields
Low Ham
Hestercombe
West Monkton
Parson's Cider
West Newton
A361
Athelney
Stathe
Aller
Upper Cheddon
Bishops Lydeard
Durston
East Lyng
Wearne
Kelways Cottage
Pitney
Cheddon Fitzpaine
West Lyng
B3153
Monkton Heathfield
Creech Heathfield
River Tone
Stoke St.Gregory
Oath
R. Parrett
Pict's Hill
Staplecombe
Tanpits Cider Farm
Taunton
Langport
1645
Staplegrove
North End
Charlton
Willows & Wetlands
Meare Green
West Sedgemoor
West Sedge Moor
Portfield
A372
Bathpool
Bridgwater & Taunton Canal
Huntham
Huish Episcopi
Pibsbury
A358
Taunton
2
Creech St.Michael
North Curry
Burton Pynsent
Curry Rivel
Priest's House
R. Yeo
Ham
Knapp
Ruishton
A378
1
Drayton
Muchelney
Cricket
25
A358
Helland
Swell Wood
Muchelney Abbey
Muchelney Ham
Bishop's Hull
Henlade
Thornfalcon
Newport
10
Swell
Midelney Manor
TAUNTON
Haydon
Fivehead
Thorney
River Parrett
A378
Wrantage
Midelney
Town Tree Nature
Stoke St.Mary
Trull
Shoreditch
Meare Green
Fivehead Arable Fields
Bowdens Farm Smokery
Staplehay
Orchard Portman
Curry Mallet
Hambridge
M5
Taunton
Thurlbear
Thurlbear Wood
River
Isle Brewers
Lock-Up
Kingsbury Episcopi
Duddlestone
West Hatch
Fivehead
B3170
Beercrocombe
Isle Abbotts
Stembridge
Coat
Fulwood
Hatch Beauchamp
Westport
Westport Canal
20
Boon's Copse
Burrow
Burrow Hill Cider
Corfe
Slough Green
Hatch Green
B3168
Barrington Court
East Lambrook
Pitminster
New Cross
Blagdon Hill
Bickenhall
West Lambrook
East Lambrook Manor
Stewley
Puckington
NT
Staple Fitzpaine
Abbey Hill
A358
Mid Lambrook
Curland
Ilton
Ilford
Barrington
Compton Durville
South Petherton
Ashill
Rapps
Curland Common
Windmill Hill
Stocklinch
Shepton Beauchamp
Holman Clavel
Staple Hill
Castle Neroche
Moor
A303
Ashwell
Hurcott
Over Stratton
Yarty Moor
Broadway
Horton Cross
Winterhay Green
Seavington St.Michael
Blackwater
Hare
Whitelackington
2
Wigborough
Robin Hood's Butts
Dommett Wood
Horton
Herne Hill
Ilminster
Seavington St.Mary
Otterford
Blindmoor
Lopen
Birchwood
13
Buckland St.Mary
Ham
Donyatt
Bishopwood Meadows
A303
Kingstone
A356
Otterhead Lakes
10
Dowlish Ford
Old Chard Canal
Bishopswood
Street Ash
Sea
Allowenshay
Dinnington
Royston Water
Newtown
Peasmarsh
Dowlish Wake
Merriott
Robin Hood's Butts
Beetham
Perry's Cider Mills
Hinton St. George
B3170
Northay
Hornsbury Mill
Knowle St.Giles
Cricket Malherbie
Lower Severalls
Combe St.Nicholas
Chillington
Broadshard
Marsh
Whitestaunton
Clayhanger
Hornsbury
Wall Brook
Bincombe Beeches
Chardleigh Green
Wadeford
Chaffcombe
Cudworth
Chard Reservoir
Howley
Cuttiford's Door
Chard Res.
Roundham
A30
Heritage Centre
A303
Crimchard
Lydmarsh
Purtington
Newcott
A30
Cricket St.Thomas
Crewkerne
The Amazing Maize Maze
Chard
Hewish
Yarcombe
Bickham Wood
Wambrook
CHARD
Misterton
Crawley
A30
Wildlife Park at Cricket St Thomas
Woolminstone
B3165
A30
Forton
B3162
Street
Ferne Animal Sanctuary
6
Wayford
A3066
River Yarty
Burridge
Whatley
Winsham
Clapton
Tatworth
B3167
Seaborough
Perry Street
Bridge
River Axe
Netherhay
Mosterton
3
South Chard
Drimpton
Stockland
Furley
Holy City
Chard Junction
Forde Abbey
Laymore
Littlewindsor
Chardstock
B3162
Horn Ash
Greenham
Millhayes
B3162
Shore Bottom
Chilson
Membury Castle
Tytherleigh
Thorncombe
Blackdown
Heathstock
Membury
Broadwindsor
Birchill
Hursey
Holditch
Hewood
Burstock
Alston
A358
Lower Holditch
B3165
Cotleigh
Beckford
Churchill
South Common
Pilsden Pen
Craft & Design Centre
Ham
Wadbrook
Turfmoor
Blackwater River
277
B3164
272
Burstock Down
Smallridge
Birdsmoorgate
Stoke Abbott
Pilsden Pen
Dalwood
Hawkchurch
Marshalsea
Wilmington
Bettiscombe
Burrow Farm
Loughwood Meeting Ho.
25
Axminster
Weycroft
D
Pilsdon
Blackney
North Bowood
Marshwood
Widworthy
B3165
Lambert's Castle
South Bowood
Umborne
Axminster
Monkwood
Axminster
Fishpond Bottom
Shute
Kilmington
B3261
Blackpool Corner
Shute Barton
Coney's Castle
Marshwood Castle
Filford
Seaton Junction
Abbey Gate
Raymond's Hill
Hampton
A35
Monkton Wyld
Broadoak
Salwayash

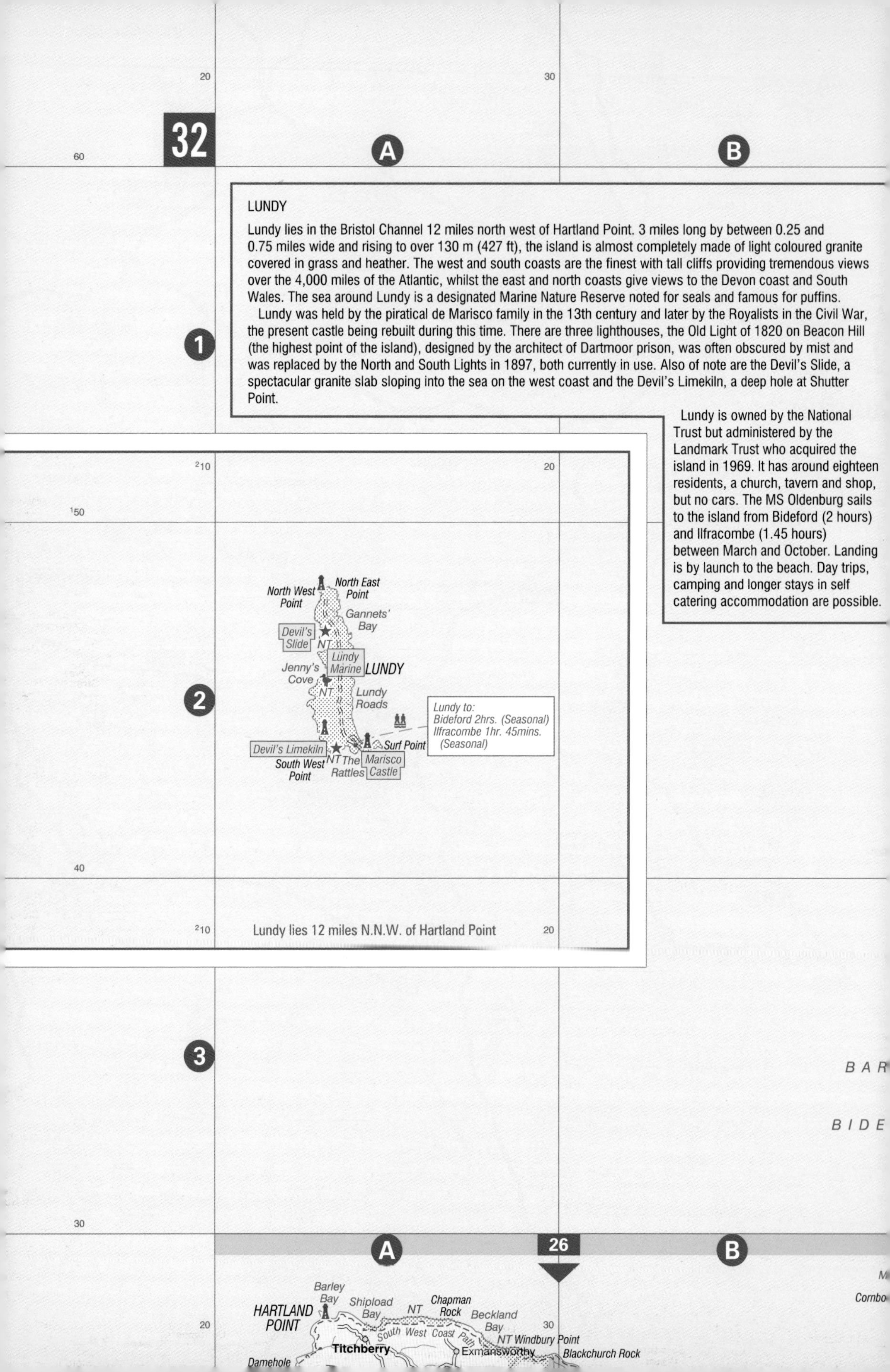

LUNDY

Lundy lies in the Bristol Channel 12 miles north west of Hartland Point. 3 miles long by between 0.25 and 0.75 miles wide and rising to over 130 m (427 ft), the island is almost completely made of light coloured granite covered in grass and heather. The west and south coasts are the finest with tall cliffs providing tremendous views over the 4,000 miles of the Atlantic, whilst the east and north coasts give views to the Devon coast and South Wales. The sea around Lundy is a designated Marine Nature Reserve noted for seals and famous for puffins.

Lundy was held by the piratical de Marisco family in the 13th century and later by the Royalists in the Civil War, the present castle being rebuilt during this time. There are three lighthouses, the Old Light of 1820 on Beacon Hill (the highest point of the island), designed by the architect of Dartmoor prison, was often obscured by mist and was replaced by the North and South Lights in 1897, both currently in use. Also of note are the Devil's Slide, a spectacular granite slab sloping into the sea on the west coast and the Devil's Limekiln, a deep hole at Shutter Point.

Lundy is owned by the National Trust but administered by the Landmark Trust who acquired the island in 1969. It has around eighteen residents, a church, tavern and shop, but no cars. The MS Oldenburg sails to the island from Bideford (2 hours) and Ilfracombe (1.45 hours) between March and October. Landing is by launch to the beach. Day trips, camping and longer stays in self catering accommodation are possible.

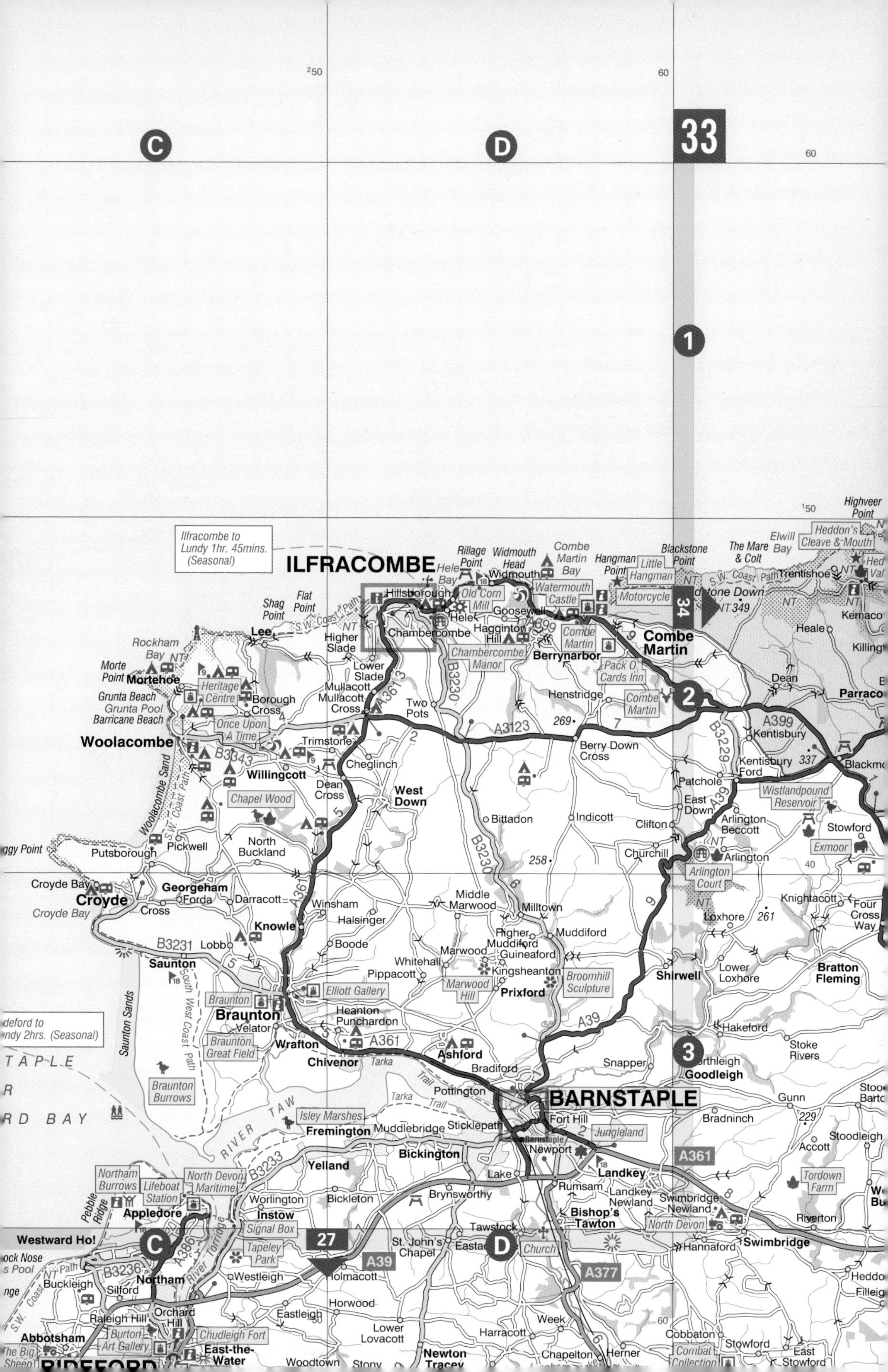

250
60
C
D
33
60
1
150
Highveer Point
Heddon's Cleave & Mouth
Elwill Bay
The Mare & Colt
Blackstone Point
Hangman Point
Little Hangman
Combe Martin Bay
Widmouth Head
Rillage Point
Hele Bay
Ilfracombe to Lundy 1hr. 45mins. (Seasonal)
ILFRACOMBE
Widmouth
Hillsborough
Old Corn Mill
Watermouth Castle
Motorcycle
34
Holdstone Down
NT 349
Trentishoe
S.W. Coast Path
NT
Kemacott
Heale
Killington
Shag Point
Flat Point
S.W. Coast Path
NT
Goosewell
Hele
Chambercombe
Hagginton Hill
A399
Combe Martin
Combe Martin
Lee
Higher Slade
Chambercombe Manor
Berrynarbor
Pack O' Cards Inn
Rockham Bay
NT
Morte Point
Mortehoe
Grunta Beach
Grunta Pool
Barricane Beach
Heritage Centre
Borough Cross
Lower Slade
Mullacott
Mullacott Cross
A3613
B3230
Two Pots
Henstridge
Combe Martin
2
Dean
Parracombe
Once Upon A Time
Woolacombe
B3343
Trimstone
A3123
269
7
Berry Down Cross
B3229
A399
Kentisbury
Kentisbury Ford
337
Blackmoor
Willingcott
Cheglinch
Dean Cross
West Down
Patchole
East Down
Wistlandpound Reservoir
Chapel Wood
Woolacombe Sand
S.W. Coast Path
Bittadon
Indicott
Clifton
A39
Arlington Beccott
Stowford
Baggy Point
Putsborough
Pickwell
North Buckland
258
Churchill
NT
Arlington
Exmoor
40
Arlington Court
Croyde Bay
Croyde
Croyde Bay
Georgeham
Forda
Cross
Darracott
A361
Winsham
Halsinger
Middle Marwood
Milltown
B3230
NT
Loxhore
261
Knightacott
Four Cross Way
Knowle
Boode
Higher Muddiford
Muddiford
B3231
Lobb
Saunton
Marwood
Guineaford
Whitehall
Kingsheanton
Shirwell
Lower Loxhore
Bratton Fleming
South West Coast Path
Pippacott
Marwood Hill
Broomhill Sculpture
Braunton
Elliott Gallery
Prixford
Bideford to Lundy 2hrs. (Seasonal)
Saunton Sands
Braunton
Velator
Heanton Punchardon
A39
Hakeford
Braunton Great Field
Wrafton
A361
Ashford
3
Stoke Rivers
TAPLE
R
RD BAY
Chivenor
Tarka
Bradiford
Snapper
Northleigh
Goodleigh
Braunton Burrows
Tarka Trail
Pottington
BARNSTAPLE
Gunn
Stoodleigh Barton
RIVER TAW
Isley Marshes
Fremington
Muddlebridge
Sticklepath
Fort Hill
Jungleland
Bradninch
229
Stoodleigh
Barnstaple
Newport
Accott
B3233
Yelland
Bickington
A361
Landkey
Tordown Farm
Northam Burrows
Lifeboat Station
North Devon Maritime
Lake
Rumsam
Landkey Newland
Swimbridge Newland
West Buckland
Pebble Ridge
Appledore
Worlington
Instow
Bickleton
Brynsworthy
Bishop's Tawton
North Devon
Riverton
Westward Ho!
Signal Box
27
Tawstock
C
Tapeley Park
St. John's Chapel
Eastacott
D
Church
Hannaford
Swimbridge
Rock Nose
s Pool
A386
River Torridge
B3236
A39
A377
Heddon
Filleigh
Buckleigh
Silford
Northam
Westleigh
Holmacott
Orchard Hill
Horwood
Eastleigh
50
60
Raleigh Hill
Week
Abbotsham
Burton Art Gallery
Chudleigh Fort
Lower Lovacott
Harracott
Cobbaton
Combat Collection
Stowford
East Stowford
The Big Sheep
BIDEFORD
East-the-Water
Woodtown
Stony
Newton Tracey
Chapelton
Herner

34
A
B
1
2
3
33
28
LYNTON
Lynmouth
Lynmouth Bay
Foreland Point
Countisbury Cove
Kipscombe Hill
Countisbury
Watersmeet
Lee Bay
Woody Bay
Martinhoe Beacon Roman Fortlet
Highveer Point
Heddon's Cleave & Mouth
Heddon Valley
Elwill Bay
The Mare & Colt
Trentishoe
Holdstone Down
Blackstone Point
Hangman Point
Little Hangman
Combe Martin Bay
Widmouth Head
Watermouth Castle
Combe Martin
Berrynarbor
Pack O' Cards Inn
Goosewell
Hagginton Hill
Henstridge
Berry Down Cross
Kentisbury
Kentisbury Ford
Blackmoor Gate
Parracombe
Churchtown
Lynton & Barnstaple Railway
Martinhoe Common
Martinhoe Cross
Kemacott
Killington
Heale
Dean
Bodley
Lynbridge
Cherrybridge
Barbrook
West Lyn
East Ilkerton
West Ilkerton
Bridge Ball
Cheriton
Wilsham
Leeford
Brendon
Rockford
Tippacott
Malmsmead
Shilstone Hill
Brendon Common
Furzehill
Shallowford
EXMOOR FOREST
Chapman Barrows
Longstone
Hoar Oak Tree
Col. R.H. Maclaren
Pinkworthy Pond
The Chains
River Exe
Challacombe
Barton Town
Sloley Stone
Shoulsbury Castle
River Barle
Simonsbath
Fortescue
Setta Barrow
Western Common
Five Barrows
Kingsford Gate
Kinsford Water
Wistlandpound Reservoir
Stowford
Exmoor
Patchole
East Down
Arlington Beccott
Arlington
Arlington Court
Clifton
Churchill
Loxhore
Knightacott
Four Cross Way
Lower Loxhore
Bratton Fleming
Shirwell
Leworthy
Lydcott
Holewater
Bittadon
Indicott
Milltown
Muddiford
Higher Muddiford
Guineaford
Kingsheanton
Broomhill Sculpture
Prixford
Bradiford
Snapper
Northleigh
Goodleigh
Hakeford
Stoke Rivers
Brayfordhill
Brayford
High Bray
North Radworthy
North Heasley
Heasley Mill
South Radworthy
BARNSTAPLE
Fort Hill
Jungleland
Newport
Landkey
Lake
Rumsam
Landkey Newland
Swimbridge Newland
Bishop's Tawton
North Devon
Tawstock
Eastacombe
Church
Hannaford
Swimbridge
Bradninch
Gunn
Stoodleigh Barton
Stoodleigh
Accott
Tordown Farm
West Buckland
East Buckland
Charles
Charles Bottom
Popham
Riverton
Flitton Oak
Millbrook
North Molton
Twitchen
Heddon
Castle Hill
Filleigh
Stag's Head
Week
Harracott
Cobbaton
Stowford
East Stowford
Chapelton
Herner
Combat Collection
Quince Honey Farm
Mornacott
Sheepwash
A39
A399
A3123
B3229
B3230
B3358
B3223
A361
A377
B3226
TOLL
NT
60
70
150
349
337
309
269
258
261
480
475
493
405
342
229
287
435

35
36
29
C
D
1
2
3
90
300
60
150
Yellow Stone
Ivy Stone
Porlock Weir Scenic Toll Road
Gore Point
Porlock Bay
TOLL
St. Beuno Church
Porlock Weir
Porlock Scenic Toll Road
Hurlstone Point
Selworthy Sand
Minehead Bluff
South West Coast Path
Bossington
Porlock
Exmoor Falconry
Lynch
Allerford
Selworthy
Burgundy Chapel
Greenaleigh Point
North Hill
MINEHEAD
West Somerset Railway
Higher Town
Woodcombe
Bratton
Periton
Minehead
Robber's
Oareford
West Porlock
Hawkcombe
Piles Watermill
A39
436
Whit Stones
Porlock Stone Circle
Horner Packhorse
Horner Wood
Horner
Horner Water
Tivington
Alcombe
Yarn Market
Car
Butter Cross
Dovecote
Dunster
Marsh Street
BLUE ANCHOR BAY
Home Farm
413
Outer Alscott
Dunkery & Horner Wood
Stoke Pero
Luccombe
Cloutsham
Huntscott
Wootton Courtenay
River Avill
Dunster Watermill
Joaney How & Robin How Burial Cairns
Gallox
Carhampton
Blue Anchor
Blue Anchor Railway
Chapel Cleeve
B3191
Kentsford House
Alderman's Barrow
Dunkery Hill
Burrow
Bat's Castle
Timberscombe
Nutcombe Bottom
Old Cleeve
Washford
519
Dunkery Beacon
A396
Withycombe
Bilbrook
S&DR
Pill River
Hungerford
Torre
MOOR
Torre Cider
Rodhuish
381
Monkham Hill
Beggearn Huish
Lower Roadwater
Newland
Edgcott
B3224
Cutcombe
Wheddon Cross
Luckwell Bridge
Exford
361
Kersham Hill
Luxborough
Kingsbridge
Roadwater
B3190
386
NATIONAL
River Exe
B3223
BRENDON HILLS
Treborough
Chidgley
Leighland Chapel
Landacre
River Quarme
Packhorse
428
Withypool Common
Withypool
Winsford Hill
426
Winsford
Wambarrows
Gupworthy
PARK
Caratacus Stone
Exton
Week
Bridgetown
Withiel Florey
SOMERSET
DEVON
Liscombe
South Hill
361
Blagdon Hill
332
Clatworthy Reservoir
Brompton Regis
Hurscombe
Tarr Steps
Woolcotts
Round Hill
Wimbleball Lake
Hancock Stone
Hawkridge
WIMBLEBALL LAKE
Huish Champflower
Huish Moor
West Anstey Common
B3223
Dulverton
Upton
355
Haddon Hill
River Haddeo
B3190
Heydon Hill
301
West Anstey
Guildhall Heritage Centre
B3222
Packhorse
Battleton
River Barle
Bury
Skilgate
Chipstable
Lee
Bottreaux Mill
Yeo Mill
East
Blackwell

36
35
30
BRIDGWA
BAY
BLUE ANCHOR BAY
MINEHEAD
WATCHET
Alcombe
Dunster
Carhampton
Timberscombe
Old Cleeve
Washford
Williton
Sampford Brett
Bicknoller
Stogumber
Crowcombe
Kilve
Holford
West Quantoxhead
East Quantoxhead
Quantock's Head
St. Audrie's Bay
Doniford
Five Bells
Chapel Cleeve
Blue Anchor
Greenaleigh Point
Higher Town
Periton
Woodcombe
Bratton
Wootton Courtenay
Burrow
Withycombe
Bilbrook
Rodhuish
Hungerford
Torre
Beggearn Huish
Lower Roadwater
Roadwater
Yarde
Monksilver
Luxborough
Kingsbridge
Treborough
Leighland Chapel
Chidgley
Monkham Hill
BRENDON HILLS
QUANTOCK HILLS
Elworthy
Rook's Nest
Brompton Ralph
Tolland
Lydeard St.Lawrence
Gupworthy
Withiel Florey
Blagdon Hill
Brompton Regis
Woolcotts
Clatworthy Reservoir
Clatworthy
Huish Champflower
Langley Marsh
Langley
Whitefield
Wiveliscombe
Pitsford Hill
Tarr
Pyleigh
Chapel Leigh
Northway
Fitzhead
Halse
Croford
Preston Bowyer
Heathfield
Ford
Hartswell
Chipstable
Skilgate
Bury
Hartford
Haddon Hill
WIMBLEBALL LAKE
Upton
Heydon Hill
VALE OF TAUNTON DEANE
Bishops Lydeard
Combe Florey
East Combe
Heathfield
West Bagborough
Terrill
Seven Ash
Triscombe
Flaxpool
Lower Vexford
Higher Vexford
Willett
Halsway
Kingswood
Newton
Vellow
Escott
Capton
Woolston
Nether Stowey
Over Stowey
Adscombe
Aley
Aisholt
Plainsfield
Dodington
Stringston
Kilton
Lilstock
Burton
Cothelstone
Toulton
East Lydeard
West Somerset Railway
North Hill
Butter Cross
Dovecote
Gallox
Bat's Castle
Nutcombe Bottom
Home Farm
Daws Castle
Blue Anchor Railway
Kentsford House
Tropiquaria
Orchard Mill
Bakelite
S&DR
Cleeve Abbey
Torre Cider
Combe Sydenham
Combe Sydenham Watermill
Elworthy Cottage
Trendle Ring
Heddon Oak
Church House
Triscombe Stone
Wills Neck
Great Wood
Quantock
Holford-Kelting
Hinkley Point
Permanent Way
Gaulden Manor
Blazes Fire
Clatworthy Reservoir
Hurscombe
Wimbleball Lake
Huish Moor
Packhorse
Dunster
Watermill
Yarn Market
Boat
A39
A396
A358
B3191
B3190
B3188
B3224
B3227
60
150
40
30
300
10
381
361
332
355
384

37
WESTON-SUPER-MARE
Sand Bay
Kewstoke
Birnbeck Island
Weston Woods
Worlebury Hill
109
Worle
St. Georges
Puxton
Congresbury
Marine Lake
Knightstone
Heritage Cen
Time Machine
Milton
Weston Milton
Worle
West Wick
Brinsea
Pier
Kidscove
Steep Holm
Weston Bay
Great Weston Train Experience
Helicopt
Court Farm
Stonebridge
Churchill
Banwell
Sandford
Locking
Sprat Beach
Fiddler's Point
Weston
Howe Rock
Black Rock
Brean Down Fort
Brean Down
NT
Black Point
Uphill
Oldmixon
Hutton
Knightcott
Dolebury Warren
Winscombe
Rowberrow
Shipham
Sidcot
Bleadon Hill
Christon
175
Lox Yeo River
Bleadon
Barton
Bleadon Level
Forgotten World
Crook Peak
191
211
233
Loxton
Compton Bishop
Cross
Brean
Animal Farm Adventure Park
Eastertown
King John's Hunting Lodge
Axbridge
Cheddar Reservoir
Cheddar
Lympsham
Biddisham
Axe
River
East Rhyne
Pitland Rhyne
Wick
Edingworth
Lower Weare
Weare
Cheddar Yeo
Berrow Flats
Berrow Dunes
SEDGEMOOR
Tarnock
Badgworth
Berrow
East Brent
Rooks Bridge
Brinscombe
Gore Sand
Brent Knoll
Stone Allerton
Alston Sutton
Clewer
Middle Burnham
Battleborough
Ashton
Allerton Moor
Crickham
BURNHAM-ON-SEA
Edithmead
Chapel Allerton
Vole
Middle Stoughton
Cocklake
Chisel Rocks
Burnham
Level
Northwick
West Stoughton
Coombes Cider
Mark
Blackford
Wedmore
Stert Island
Apex
Rich's Cider
Highbridge
Mark Causeway
Yarrow
Sand
Hinkley Point Power Stations
Bridgwater Bay
Alstone
Highbridge & Burnham
Bason Bridge
Watchfield
Westham
Heath House
Mark Moor
Bagley
Stolford
Steart
Huntspill
Secret World
River Brue
Mudgley
North Drain
Westhay Moor
Somerset Levels & Moors
East Huntspill
Tadham Moor
Wick
Stretcholt
West Huntspill
Huntspill Level
Huntspill River
Huntspill Moor
Stockland Bristol
RIVER PARRETT
Burtle
Lake Villages (site of)
Otterhampton
Black Ditch
Chilton Moor
Combwich
Pawlett Hams
Pawlett
Westhay
Fish House
Puriton Level
Edington Heath
Oxenpill
Shapwick Heath
Meare
Peat Moors
Coultings
Woolavington
Puriton
Dunball
Catcott Heath
Cossington
Fiddington
Rodway
Edington
Horsey Level
Chilton Polden
Cannington
Bawdrip
Catcott
College Heritage
Perry Green
Chilton Trinity
Bradney
Stawell
Shapwick
Ashford Res.
Bradley Green
Polden Hills
Wembdon
Somerset Brick & Tile
Ashcott
Charlynch
Slape Cross
Spaxton
Sydenham
Chedzoy
Moorlynch
Pedwell
Four Forks
Durleigh Res.
Northfield
Bridgwater
Sutton Mallet
Moorlinch
Greinton
Pightley
Admiral Blake
Hawkridge Res.
Brook
Durleigh
Hamp
Sedgemoor
1685
Battle
King's Sedgemoor Drain
Enmore
Bussex
BRIDGWATER
Westonzoyland
Rhode
Andersfield
Temple of Harmony
Goathurst
Woolmersdon
Huntworth
Greylake
King's Sedge Moor
Huntstile
Andersea
Weston Level
King's Sedge Moor
North Petherton
Fyne Court
Fordgate
Pumping Station
Middlezoy
Heaven's Gate Farm
Henley
Thorngrove
Broomfield
Northmoor Green or Moorland
Earlake Moor
Othery
High Ham
Clavelshay
Shearston
North Newton
Burrow Mump
Beer
Thurloxton
North Moor
Aller & Beer
Kingston St.Mary
Bankland
Burrowbridge
Pathe
Stembridge
Fulford
Adsborough
31
Maunsel Canal Centre
Hestercombe
West Monkton
West Newton
Parson's Cider
Athelney
Stathe
Aller
Bowdens
Prospect Fields
Low Ham
Upper Cheddon
Durston
East Lyng
Pitney
Cheddon Fitzpaine
Canal
West Lyng
Wearne
Kelways Cottage
Monkton Heathfield
Creech Heathfield
River Tone
R. Parrett
Stoke St.Gregory
Oath
Pict's Hill
Langport
1645
Staplecombe
Tanpits Cider Farm
Willows & Wetlands
Staplegrove
North End
Charlton
Meare Green
West Sedgemoor
Portfield
Huish
M5
A38
A368
A371
A370
A39
A372
A361
B3140
B3139
B3141
B3151
B3153
B3133
B3340
B3339
S
C
D
1
2
3
22
23
24

TOWN PLANS

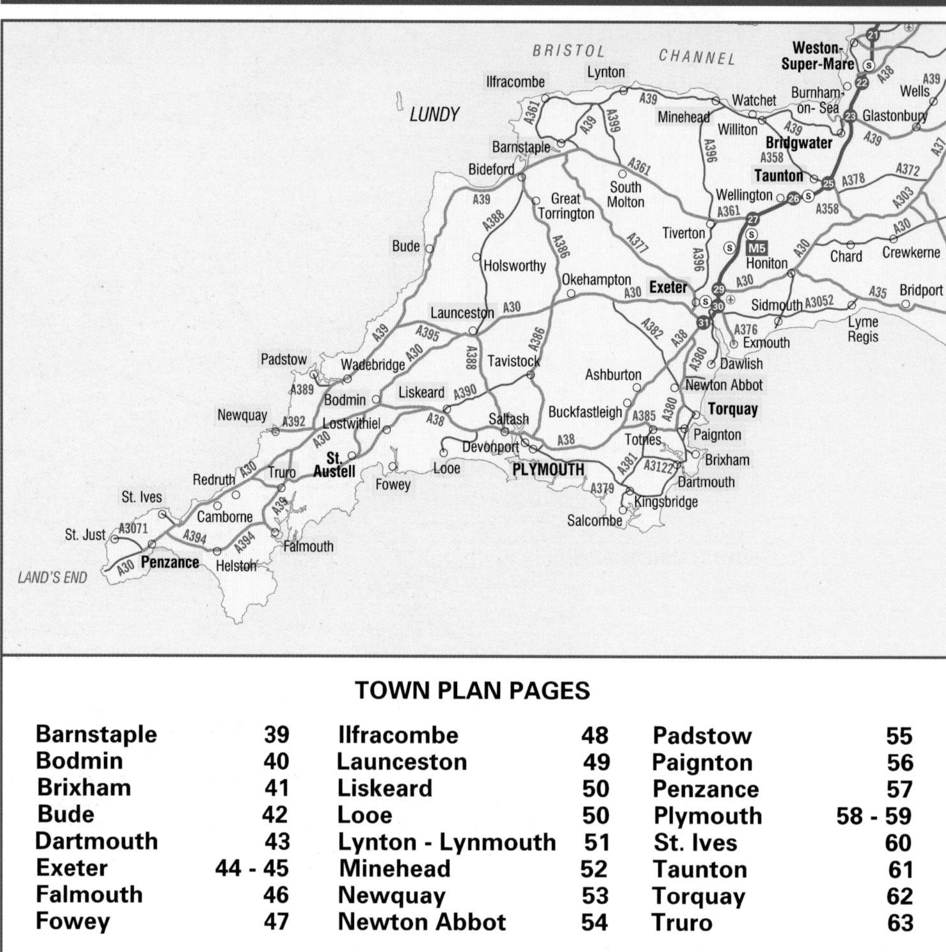

TOWN PLAN PAGES

TOWN PLAN ONLY SYMBOLS

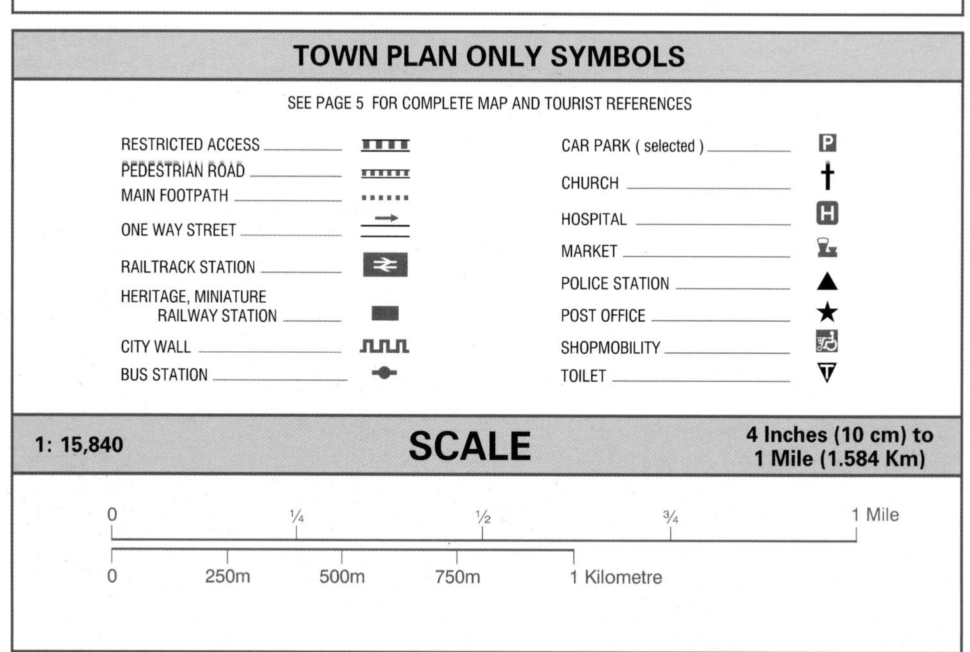

BARNSTAPLE

Barnstaple is a market town and former port situated on the tidal River Taw where it is crossed by the widened 13th century sixteen arch Long Bridge. The town traded in Barum ware pottery and this is still made at Brannams Pottery (on Roundswell Industrial Estate to the south west). There is a Pannier Market in the large Market House on Butchers Row and on Paternoster Row nearby is St Anne's Chapel, an early chantry chapel once used as a grammar school. A pleasant riverside walk runs along the quay, off The Strand, leading to Queen Anne's Walk, a colonnaded arcade of 1796 with a statue of Queen Anne.

PLACES OF INTEREST

Tourist Information Centre
(All year) - The Square.
Tel: 01271 375000

◆ BARNSTAPLE CASTLE- Built in the reign of William the Conqueror, the mound & traces of the moat are all that remain of the former Norman castle. Tuly Street. ◆ BARNSTAPLE HERITAGE CENTRE - Displays recounting Barnstaple's heritage set in magnificent Grade 1 listed building on the historic riverfront. Queen Anne's Walk, The Strand. ◆ BARNSTAPLE & NORTH DEVON, MUSEUM OF - Various collections detailing the history of North Devon. Highlights include pottery, furniture, the Regimental Collection of the Royal Devon Yeomanry and the Tarka Gallery. North Devon Athenaeum, The Square.
◆ TARKA TRAIL - Long distance path forming a figure-of-eight circuit over 180 miles. The section from Braunton to Meeth (via Barnstaple & Bideford) allows for both walkers & cyclists.

ENTERTAINMENT

◆ Cinemas - Boutport Street.
◆ Theatres - Queens Theatre, Boutport Street.

SPORT & LEISURE

◆ Parks & Gardens - Castle Mound, Tuly Street. Pilton Park, Pilton Causeway. Rock Park, New Road.
◆ Sports Centres - North Devon Leisure Centre, Seven Brethren Bank, Sticklepath. Park School Community Sports Hall, Park Lane (SE Barnstaple).
◆ Swimming Pools - North Devon Leisure Centre (as above).
◆ Ten-Pin Bowling - Lets Go Superbowl, Braunton Road.

Hartland Point

Clovelly

BODMIN

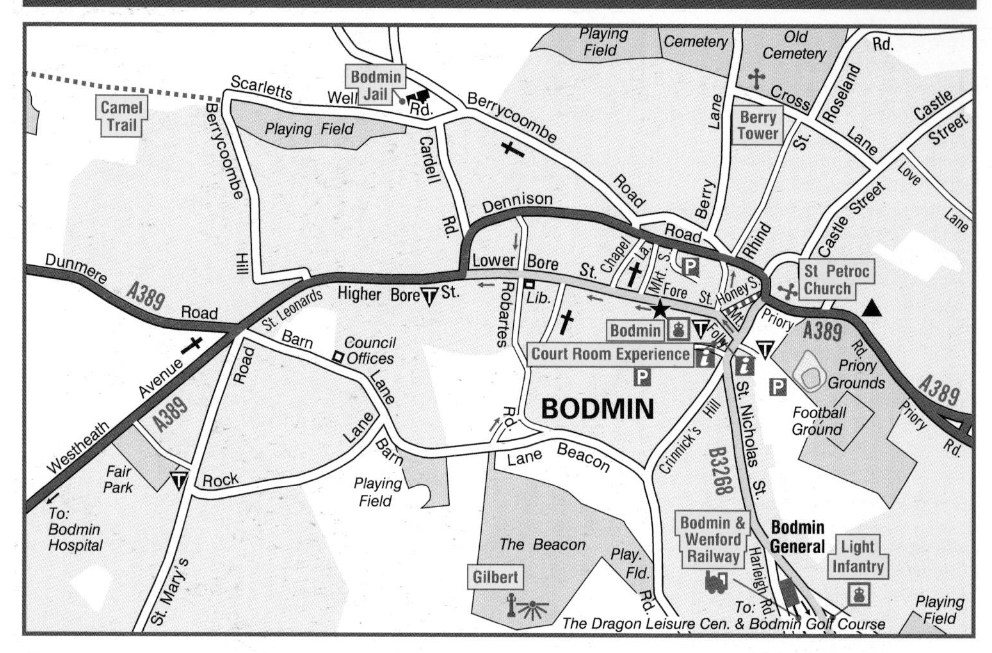

Bodmin, situated on a hillside site, is the former county town of Cornwall. The town had an important priory until the Dissolution. Of note are the neo-classical granite Shire Hall (the former County Assize Court building of 1838 on Mount Folly last used in 1988 - see below), the county prison and St Petroc's Church (see below). The Beacon has panoramic views.

PLACES OF INTEREST

Tourist Information Centre (All year)- The Shire Hall, Mount Folly. Tel: 01208 76616

◆ BERRY TOWER - Remains of tower of St Annes Priory. Old Cemetery, Berry Lane. ◆ BODMIN & WENFORD RAILWAY - 6 mile standard gauge steam railway. Stations at Bodmin General, Colesloggett Halt (for Cardinham Woods), Bodmin Parkway (main line) & Boscarne Junction (for Camel Trail). Bodmin General Station, Lostwithiel Road. ◆ BODMIN JAIL - Former county prison dating back to 1776. Exhibition with recreated displays in dungeons & cells. Berrycombe Road. ◆ BODMIN MUSEUM - History of Bodmin up to the end of WWII. Costumes, domestic and farming artifacts. Mount Folly. ◆ CAMEL TRAIL - Popular 17 mile cycleway & footpath on former LSWR railway line linking Padstow, Wadebridge & Bodmin, continuing to Poley's Bridge nr. Wenfordbridge. ◆ DUKE OF CORNWALL'S LIGHT INFANTRY MUSEUM - Regimental history, military artefacts, uniforms & medals. The Keep, Victoria Barracks, Plas Newydd Avenue. ◆ GILBERT MONUMENT - 44 m (144 ft) high granite obelisk in memory of Sir Walter Raleigh Gilbert. The Beacon. ◆ ST PETROC CHURCH - Cornwall's largest church containing 12th century reliquary of St Petroc. Priory Road. ◆ SHIRE HALL COURT ROOM EXPERIENCE - Recreation of the 19th century trial, in original court building, of murderer of Charlotte Dymond whose body was found on Rough Tor in 1844. Holding cells. The Shire Hall, Mount Folly. ◆ TOWN & COUNTRYSIDE CENTRE - History, wildlife, information on Camel trail, activities, places to see in Bodmin, on Bodmin Moor & in the surrounding area. The Shire Hall, Mount Folly.

SPORT & LEISURE

◆ Parks & Gardens - Fair Park, Westheath Avenue. Priory Ground, Priory Road. The Beacon, Beacon Rd.
◆ Sports Centres - The Dragon Leisure Centre, Lostwithiel Road (S of Bodmin General Station).
◆ Swimming Pools - The Dragon Leisure Centre (as above).

Cornish Countryside

BRIXHAM

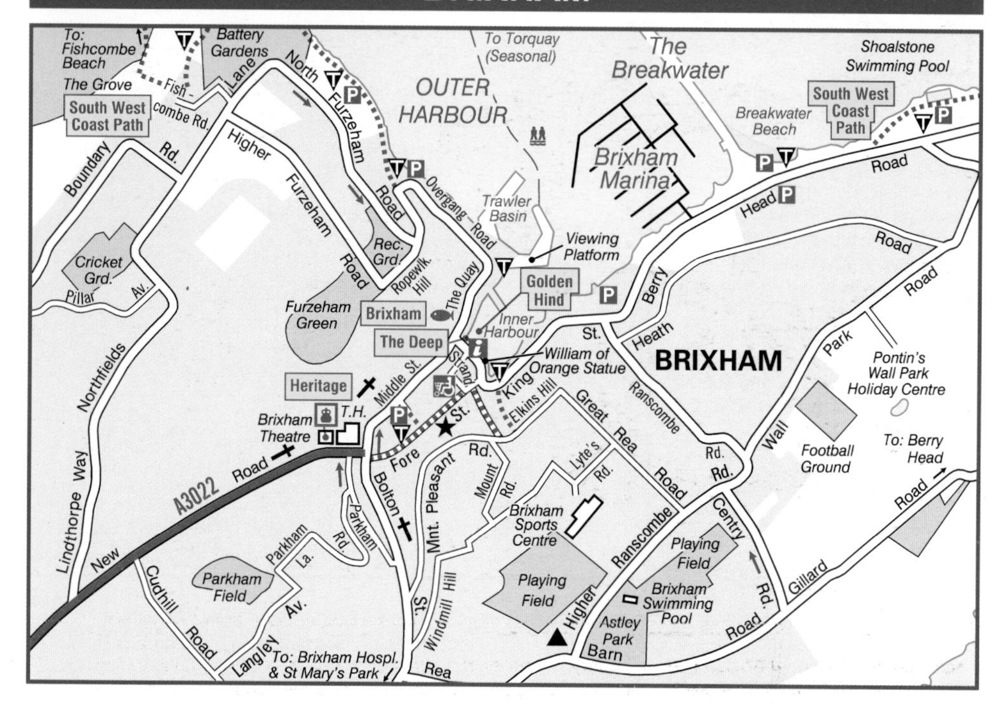

Brixham, a popular small fishing port with narrow streets, was described in 1850 as 'the largest fishery in England' and it is still an important trawler port with a busy fish market. The half mile long breakwater protects the outer harbour and Brixham Marina whilst a viewing platform on the New Pier (built in 1803/4), accessible to the public, overlooks the Trawler Basin. A statue on the Strand commemorates William of Orange's landing in Brixham in 1688 and preserved WWII gun battery emplacements can be seen in Battery Gardens.

PLACES OF INTEREST

Tourist Information Centre (All year)- The Old Market House, The Quay. Tel: 0870 707 0010

◆ BRIXHAM AQUARIUM - Marine life including sharks, octopi & eels. 12 The Quay. ◆ BRIXHAM HERITAGE MUSEUM - Local & maritime history including shipbuilding, smuggling, lifeboats, the coastguard, trawler models, pictures & costume. Bolton Cross, New Road. ◆ GOLDEN HIND, THE - Replica of Sir Francis Drake's ship on which he sailed around the world in 1577-80. Displays on life at sea. The Quay. ◆ THE DEEP - History, fables & monsters of the ocean. Re-creations of sea cave, trawler, sunken pirate ship featuring whales, mermaids & folklore. The Old Market House, The Quay.

ENTERTAINMENT

◆ Theatres - Brixham Theatre, New Road.

SPORT & LEISURE

◆ Parks & Gardens - Astley Park, Higher Ranscombe Road.
Battery Gardens, North Furzeham Road.
Furzeham Green, Higher Furzeham Road.
Parkham Field, Parkham Lane.
St Mary's Park, Upton Manor Road (S Brixham).
◆ Sports Centres - Brixham Sports Centre, Lytes Road.
◆ Swimming Pools - Brixham Swimming Pool, Higher Ranscombe Road. Shoalstone Swimming Pool, Berry Head Road.

Brixham

BUDE

Bude grew up as an agricultural trading port, serving the surrounding remote rural area, to which it was linked by the 35 mile long Bude Canal built in the 1820s. Known for its inclined planes instead of locks, the 2 miles to Helebridge survive with pleasant towpath walks. Bude later became a Victorian & Edwardian resort and it remains a popular family seaside destination. Crooklets Beach is used for surfing. The Castle (now council offices) was built in 1850 by Sir Goldsworthy Gurney, best known for his invention of incandescent lighting and the steam powered road coach.

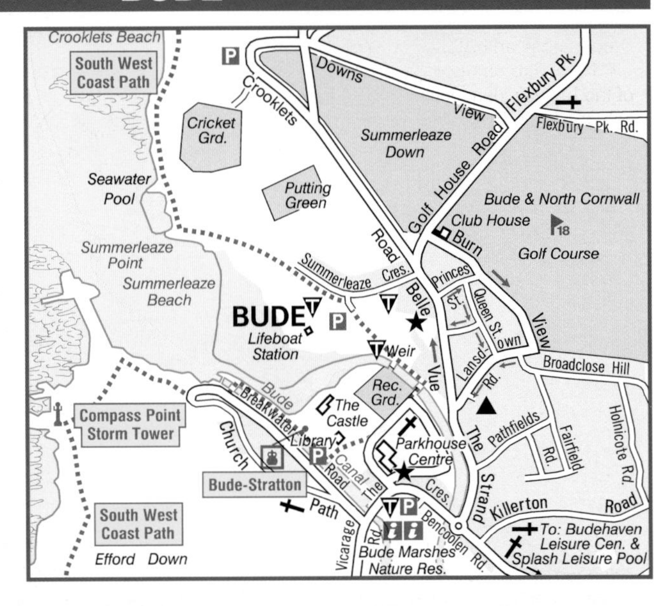

PLACES OF INTEREST

Tourist Information Centre (All year)- Bude Visitor Centre, The Crescent car park.
Tel: 01288 354240 ◆ BUDE-STRATTON MUSEUM - Displays on the Bude Canal, railway & local shipwrecks. Audio-visual. Lower Wharf. ◆ BUDE VISITOR CENTRE - Information on the natural history of the Bude area. The Crescent car park. ◆ COMPASS POINT STORM TOWER - Eight sided storm tower marked with points of the compass. Compass Point, Efford Down.

SPORT & LEISURE

- ◆ Parks & Gardens - Summerleaze Down, Crooklets Road.
- ◆ Sports Centres - Budehaven Leisure Centre, Stratton Road.
- ◆ Swimming Pools - Seawater Pool, Summerleaze Beach. Splash Leisure Pool, Stratton Road.

Coastline Cornwall

DARTMOUTH

Dartmouth is an historic port and holiday centre on the west side of the beautiful land-locked estuary of the River Dart. Once important for the export of cloth and for trade with Newfoundland, the town is characterized by narrow streets, alleyways and long flights of steps such as Horn Hill and Browns Hill (once the main packhorse route). The South Embankment quay is ideal for harbour watching and from here the foot ferry crosses to Kingswear and popular river cruises leave for Totnes, 10 miles upstream, and trips past Dartmouth Castle downstream. Buildings of note include The Butterwalk in Duke Street dating from 1635-40 with elaborately carved overhanging timbers, the colonnaded Old Market House (dating from the 1830s) in Market Square and the famous Britannia Royal Naval College of 1905.

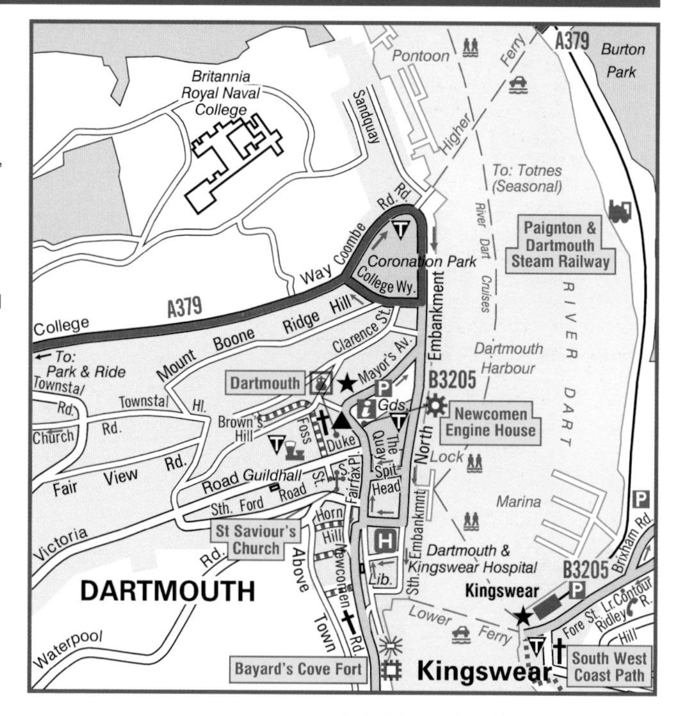

PLACES OF INTEREST

Tourist Information Centre (All year)- The Engine House, Mayor's Avenue. Tel: 01803 834224

◆ BAYARD'S COVE FORT (EH) - Small artillery fort of 1510 built to protect the harbour entrance. Riverfront, Southtown. ◆ DARTMOUTH MUSEUM - Maritime history, ship models, pictures and artifacts relating to Dartmouth & its estuary. The Butterwalk, Duke Street. ◆ NEWCOMEN ENGINE HOUSE - Engine of 1725, a memorial to Dartmouth born Thomas Newcomen, inventor of the atmospheric steam pumping engine. The Engine House, Royal Avenue Gardens, Mayor's Avenue. ◆ PAIGNTON & DARTMOUTH STEAM RAILWAY - 7 mile standard gauge steam railway using GWR engines. Stations at Kingswear, Churston, Goodrington, Paignton. Kingswear Station, Kingswear. ◆ ST SAVIOUR'S CHURCH - Noted for its 15th century ornate rood screen with painted panels of saints. Church Close.

SPORT & LEISURE

◆ Parks & Gardens - Coronation Park, North Embankment. Royal Avenue Gardens, Mayor's Avenue.

River Dart

EXETER

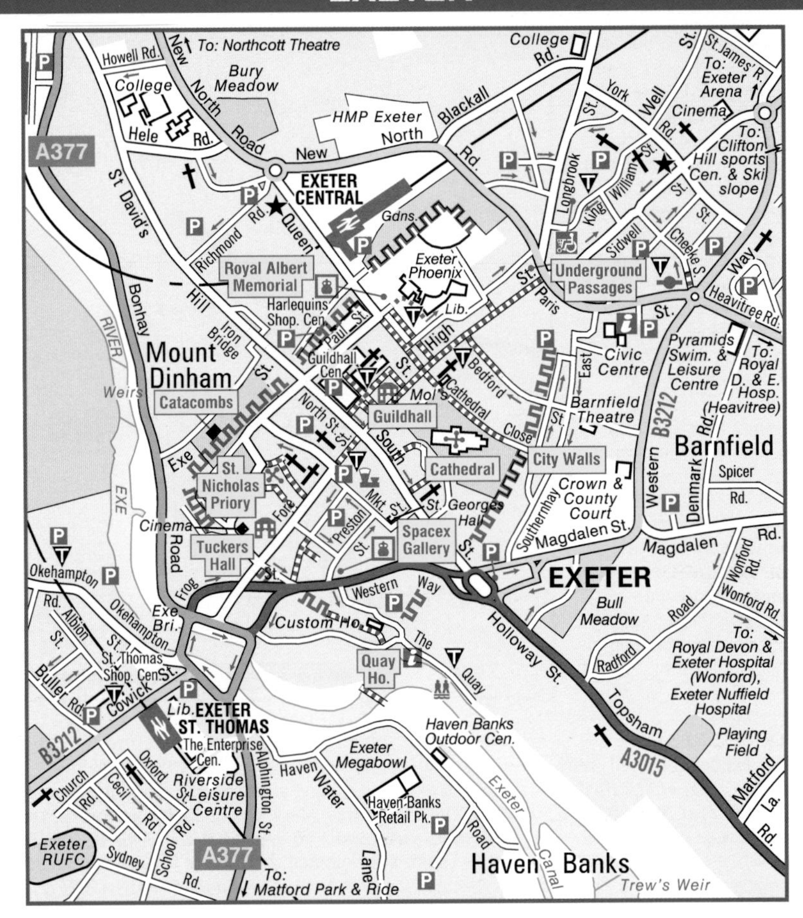

Exeter, a cathedral and university city, is the county 'town' of Devon and remains an historic city despite damage from wartime bombing raids in 1942. Of note are Fore Street, the cobbled Stepcote Hill (the only surviving medieval street in the city), Mol's Coffee House of 1596 in Cathedral Close and the Custom House of 1681 on the Quay. The city was once a major port exporting woollen cloth and is connected with the Exe estuary at Topsham by the 5 mile long Exeter Ship Canal, built in the 1560s, followed by a canalside walk. 'Exeter Historic Quayside' is now a popular waterside area with shops and restaurants.

Exeter Cathedral

Tudor Buildings, Exeter

Dart Valley

PLACES OF INTEREST

Tourist Information Centre (All year) - Civic Centre, Paris Street. Tel: 01392 265700

◆ CATACOMBS, THE - Underground catacombs of the citys 17th century old cemetery. Guided tours only (inquire at tourist information centre). Bartholomew Street East.

◆ EXETER CATHEDRAL - Symmetrical building with twin Norman towers, the peak of the Decorated Gothic style in England. Longest Gothic vaulted nave in the country. West front sculptures. Cathedral Close.

◆ EXETER CITY WALLS - Roman town wall of 200 AD rebuilt in medieval times (no gateways survive). Best sections off Southernhay West, Bartholomew Street East, Northernhay Street & Northernhay Gardens.

◆ EXETER GUILDHALL - One of the oldest municipal buildings to survive in England still in use, dating from 1330 with a pillared facade of 1593. City's silver & regalia on display. High Street.

◆ EXETER ROUGEMONT CASTLE - Early Norman gatehouse & fragments of wall remain. Crown Court of 1774 & Rougemont Gardens now occupy most of the site. Castle Street.

◆ EXETER UNDERGROUND PASSAGES - Medieval underground conduits built to supply fresh water to the city. Exhibition, audio-visual, guided tour. Britain's only subterranean waterways open to the public. Eastgate, off High Street (nr. Boots).

◆ QUAY HOUSE VISITOR CENTRE - History of the port of Exeter with models, paintings & artifacts. Audio-visual on story of Exeter from its Roman origins to the present day. 46 The Quay.

◆ ROYAL ALBERT MEMORIAL MUSEUM & ART GALLERY - Exeter silver, Devon archaeology & natural history, paintings by Devon artists, fine art, ceramics, glass. Queen Street.

◆ ST NICHOLAS PRIORY - Guest wing of an 11th century Benedictine priory with a Norman undercroft, kitchen & guest hall. The Mint, off Fore Street.

◆ SPACEX GALLERY - Changing contemporary art exhibitions. 45 Preston Street.

◆ TUCKERS HALL - Medieval guild hall of the Weavers, Fullers & Shearmen of the wool & cloth trade, with an arched braced roof of 1471. Fore Street.

ENTERTAINMENT

◆ Cinemas - Bartholomew Street West. Sidwell Street.

◆ Concerts- St Georges Hall, Market Street.

◆ Theatres- Barnfield Theatre, Barnfield Road. Exeter Phoenix Arts Centre, Bradninch Place, Gandy Street. Northcott Theatre, University of Exeter Campus, Stocker Road, St David's (N of Exeter).

SPORT & LEISURE

◆ Parks & Gardens- Bull Meadow, Bull Meadow Road. Bury Meadow, North Road. Northernhay Gardens, Queen Street. Rougemont Gardens, Castle Street.

◆ Sports Centres - Clifton Hill Sports Centre, Clifton Hill (NE Exeter). County Ground Stadium, off Cowick Street. Exeter Arena Athletic Stadium, Summer Lane (NE Exeter). Pyramids Swimming & Leisure Centre, Heavitree Road. Riverside Leisure Centre, The Plaza, Cowick Street. St James' Sports Centre, St James' High School, Summer Lane (NE Exeter). Wonford Sports Centre, Burnthouse Lane (SE Exeter).

◆ Ski Slope - Clifton Hill Sports Centre (as above).

◆ Swimming Pools - Northbrook Swimming Pool, Beacon Lane (NE Exeter). Pyramids Swimming & Leisure Centre (as above). Riverside Leisure Centre (as above).

◆ Ten Pin Bowling- Exeter Megabowl, Haven Banks Retail Park, Water Lane.

FALMOUTH

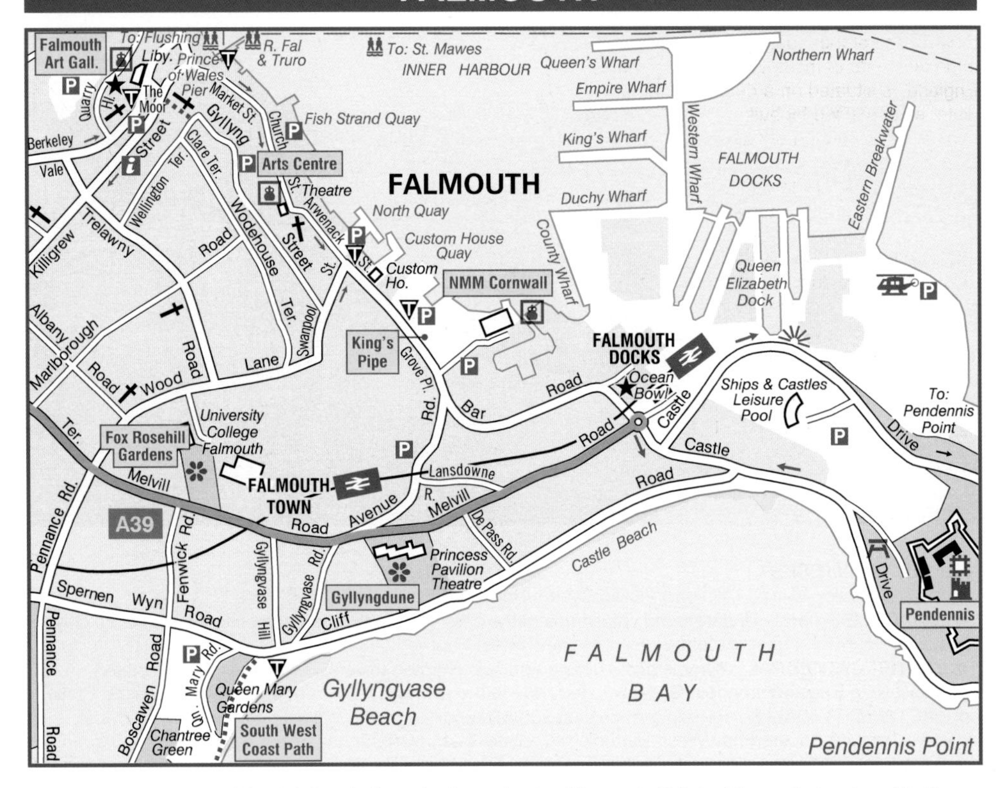

Falmouth Harbour and Carrick Roads form the largest natural haven in Britain. The port, developed in the 16th century by the Killigrew family, thrived by becoming a packet station for the Post Office between 1688 and 1852. It is now a major sailing centre with ship repair facilities centred on Falmouth Docks, best viewed from Castle Drive. Ferries to St Mawes, Flushing and along the River Fal to Truro leave from the Prince of Wales Pier. The town is noted for its gardens and parks with sub-tropical plants.

PLACES OF INTEREST

Tourist Information Centre (All year)- 28 Killigrew Street. Tel: 01326 312300

◆ FALMOUTH ART GALLERY - Changing art exhibitions in late 19th century Passmore Edwards Library. Municipal Buildings, The Moor.

◆ FALMOUTH ARTS CENTRE - Changing fine art exhibitions in four galleries. Paintings, sculpture, ceramics, photography & craft by local & national artists. 24 Church Street.

◆ FOX ROSEHILL GARDENS - 2 acre gardens containing exotic tree species including lemon, banana, eucalyptus & palms. Melvill Road.

◆ GYLLYNGDUNE GARDENS - Falmouth's finest formal gardens linked to seafront by a grotto walkway. Melvill Road.

◆ KING'S PIPE - Brick chimney once used to burn contraband tobacco. Arwenack Street.

◆ NATIONAL MARITIME MUSEUM CORNWALL - Purpose built £21.5 million outstation of the National Maritime Museum (Greenwich). Over 40 vessels. Boat, Cornwall & Environment Galleries. Viewing tower. Interactive displays. Discovery Quay.

◆ PENDENNIS CASTLE (EH) - Henry VIII castle with three storey circular keep & extensive outworks. Discovery Centre (Tudor gun-deck), WWII underground tunnels. Castle Drive.

ENTERTAINMENT

◆ Cinemas - Falmouth Arts Centre (see above).

◆ Theatres - Falmouth Arts Centre (see above). Princess Pavilion Theatre, Melvill Road.

SPORT & LEISURE

◆ Parks & Gardens - Fox Rosehill Gardens (see above). Gyllyngdune Gardens (see above). Kimberley Park, Kimberley Park Road (W Falmouth). Queen Mary Gardens, Queen Mary Road.

◆ Swimming Pools - Ships & Castles Leisure Pool, Castle Drive.

◆ Ten Pin Bowling - Ocean Bowl, Pendennis Rise.

FOWEY

Fowey, one of the most important ports of medieval England, is situated on a deep water estuary used by bulk carriers for the export of china clay from the docks upstream. Justly famous for its beautiful harbour, with colourful yachts viewable from the Town Quay, the town has associations with novelist Daphne du Maurier who lived at Ferryside in Bodinnick and scholar and novelist Sir Arthur Quiller-Couch (known by the pseudonym 'Q') who lived at The Haven, Esplanade. The 15th century castellated mansion of Place is the home of the Treffry Family.

PLACES OF INTEREST

Tourist Information Centre (All year) - 5 South Street. Tel: 01726 833616

◆ DAPHNE DU MAURIER LITERARY CENTRE - Exhibition & audio-visual display reflecting the novelists life & works. 5 South Street.
◆ FOWEY AQUARIUM - Marine aquarium exhibiting species caught locally. Old Town Hall, Town Quay.
◆ FOWEY MUSEUM - History of port of Fowey, ship models, local interest. Old Town Hall, Town Quay.
◆ HALL WALK (NT) - 16th century walk from Bodinnick to Penleath Point, where King Charles I was fired upon in 1644. (see 'Q Memorial' below) ◆ HEADLAND GARDEN - 1 1/4 ac. cliff garden. Plants & trees resistant to salt-laden gales. Sub-tropical plants. 3 Battery Lane, Polruan. ◆ OLD HOUSE OF FOYE - Reputed oldest house in Fowey, c1430. Old kitchen, beams etc. Fore Street. ◆ POLRUAN & FOWEY BLOCKHOUSES - Built in the late 15th century either side of the harbour, a chain boom was hung between the blockhouses to prevent the entry of enemy vessels. Polruan Blockhouse is best preserved. ◆ ST CATHERINE'S CASTLE (EH) - Small defensive Henry VIII coastal fort c1530. Above Readymoney Cove. ◆ SIR ARTHUR QUILLER-COUCH MEMORIAL (NT) - Monument & famous viewpoint over Fowey, estuary & Pont Pill creek. Hall Walk, Bodinnick.

SPORT & LEISURE

◆ Parks & Gardens - Squires Field, Park Road.
◆ Sports Centres - Fowey Community Leisure Centre, Windmill.

Fowey

ILFRACOMBE

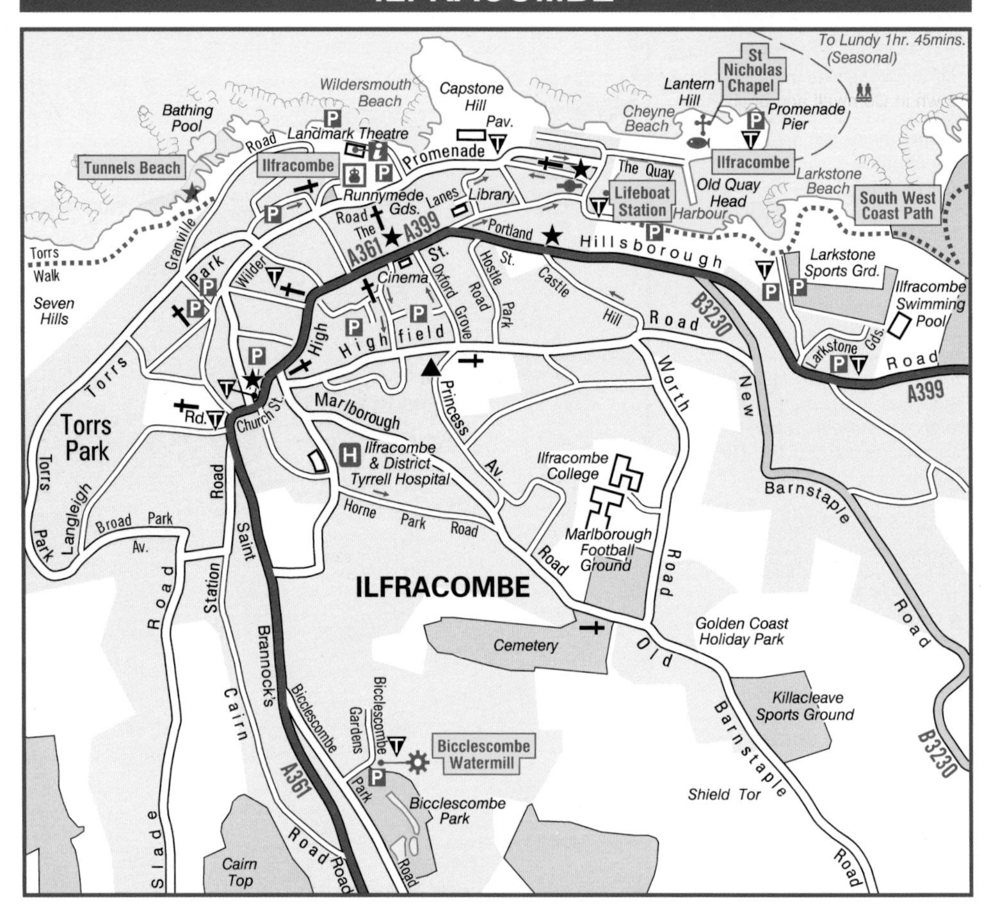

Ilfracombe, the picturesque town with its spectacular scenery and ancient harbour is North Devon's most popular seaside resort. The network of passages running from the High Street to the Sea Front known as 'The Lanes' enable the pedestrian to explore Ilfracombe along some of its oldest paths. A section has been developed into a sculpture trail with mosaics depicting various features characteristic of the town. The South West coastal path runs through Ilfracombe and the famous Torrs Walk heads out west to the village of Lee offering extensive views as you walk along the cliff top. In the summer months, the MS Oldenburg runs regular sailings to Lundy Island.

PLACES OF INTEREST

Tourist Information Centre (All year) - The Landmark Theatre, The Seafront. Tel: 01271 003001

◆ BICCLESCOMBE WATERMILL - Restored 18th century mill. Runs during the Summer for demonstration purposes only. Bicclescombe Park, Bicclescombe Gardens. ◆ ILFRACOMBE AQUARIUM - Marine life from the source of an Exmoor stream to the sea. Rockpools, marine conservation, interactive environments. The Old Lifeboat House, The Pier. ◆ ILFRACOMBE MUSEUM - Located in a building dating from 1885, this intriguing collection contains over 20,000 exhibits of natural history along with war memorabilia, paintings, photographs & Victoriana which reflect life of a bygone age. There is also a brass-rubbing centre. Runnymede Gardens, Wilder Road. ◆ LIFEBOAT STATION - Established 1828. Inflatable 'D' & Mersey Class lifeboats. Cove car park, The Quay. ◆ ST NICHOLAS CHAPEL - 14th century chapel has been used as a lighthouse to guide seafarers into the harbour since 1522. Small exhibition illustrating the history of the chapel & local area. Lantern Hill, The Quay. ◆ TUNNELS BEACH - Approximately 150 years ago, 4 tunnels were created by cutting through rock to provide access to this famous beach location. Granville Rd.

ENTERTAINMENT

◆ Cinemas - 134 High Street. Landmark Theatre, The Promenade.
◆ Theatres - Landmark Theatre (see above).

SPORT & LEISURE

◆ Parks & Gardens - Bicclescombe Park, Bicclescombe Road. Runnymede Gardens, Wilder Road.
◆ Swimming Pools - Ilfracombe Swimming Pool, Hillsborough Road.

LAUNCESTON

Launceston, an ancient medieval hill top town, was the only walled town in Cornwall and until 1835 was the county's capital. Dunheved, the old town, is dominated by the castle and has many narrow twisting streets, of note being Castle Street with its brick Georgian houses. The town once had two railway stations at Newport served by two competing companies.

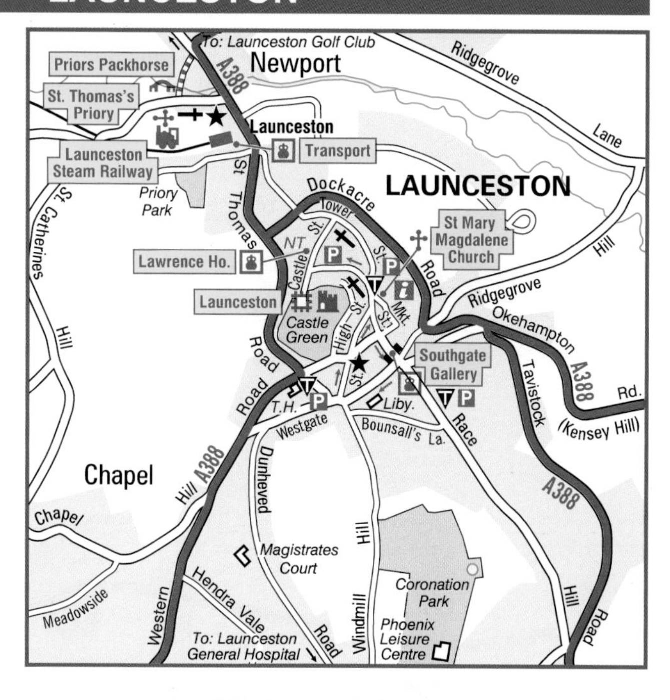

PLACES OF INTEREST

Tourist Information Centre (All year) - Market House Arcade, Market Street.
Tel: 01566 772321 / 772333

◆ LAUNCESTON CASTLE (EH) - Norman motte with shell keep & cylindrical tower providing commanding views. Castle Street.
◆ LAUNCESTON STEAM RAILWAY - 2 mile 2ft. gauge steam railway using Victorian locomotives on route of former North Cornwall line. Stations at Launceston, Hunts Crossing, Deer Park & Newmills (picnic site). Launceston Station, Newport Industrial Estate, St Thomas Road. ◆ LAUNCESTON STEAM RAILWAY TRANSPORT MUSEUM - Vintage cars, motorcycles, stationary steam engines. Launceston Steam Railway (see above).
◆ LAWRENCE HOUSE MUSEUM (NT) - Georgian house of 1753 housing museum of local history. Victorian dressing room & costumes. 9 Castle Street. ◆ PRIORS PACKHORSE BRIDGE - Ancient five arched packhorse bridge over River Kensey. Westbridge Road. ◆ ST MARY MAGDALENE CHURCH - Exterior adorned with decorative carvings (apart from tower) datings from early 16th century. Church Street.
◆ ST THOMAS'S PRIORY - Ruins of 12th century Augustinian Priory behind St Thomas's church. Riverside. ◆ SOUTHGATE GALLERY - Art gallery in room above the narrow arch of Southgate, a surviving part of the former 16th century town walls. Southgate Street.

SPORT & LEISURE

◆ Parks & Gardens - Castle Green, Castle Street. Coronation Park, Dunheved Road.
◆ Sports Centres - Phoenix Leisure Centre, Coronation Park, Dunheved Road.
◆ Swimming Pools - Phoenix Leisure Centre (as above)

Ilfracombe

LISKEARD / LOOE

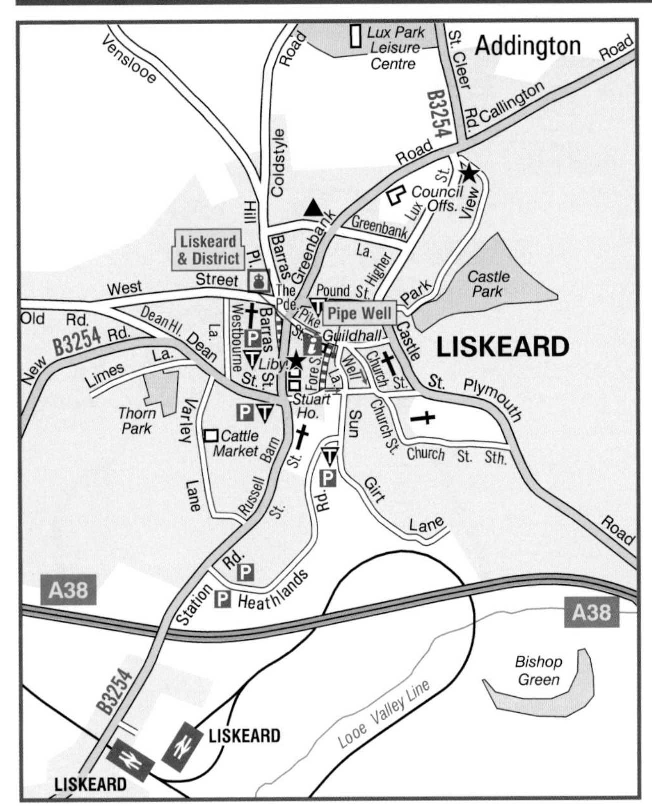

Liskeard, one of four former Stannary (or coinage) towns for the tin industry, is a busy hill top market town. The town has many fine Georgian buildings in the Parade, the 1850s Italian style Victorian Guildhall with tall clock tower in Pike Street and the late 19th century Passmore Edwards Library, together with Stuart House, in Barras Street. The Looe Valley Line is a scenic 8.5 mile branch railway line to Looe.

PLACES OF INTEREST

Tourist Information Centre (All year) - Foresters Hall, Pike Street. Tel: 01579 349148

◆ LISKEARD & DISTRICT MUS. - Local history of Liskeard. Foresters Hall, Pike Street.

◆ PIPE WELL - Four spout well never known to dry up. Well Lane.

SPORT & LEISURE

◆ Parks & Gardens - Castle Park, Castle Street. Thorn Park, Limes Lane.

◆ Sports Centres - Lux Park Leisure Centre, Coldstyle Road.

◆ Swimming Pools - Lux Park Leisure Centre (as above).

Looe is a busy fishing port famous as a shark fishing centre and is home to the Shark Angling Club of Great Britain. Situated on a narrow estuary at the confluence of the two Looe rivers it is divided into East Looe with its small narrow streets and West Looe, its quieter counterpart, linked together by a seven-arched Victorian bridge built in 1855. St George's Island, more commonly known as Looe Island, lies about a mile from the mainland and was bought in 1965 by sisters Babs and Evelyn Atkins who resided there. They bequeathed the island to the Cornwall Wildlife Trust in 2004 who now manage it as a nature reserve.
The beach near Banjo Pier is popular and a fish market is held on Buller Quay. The Looe Valley Line is a scenic 8.5 mile branch railway line to Liskeard.

PLACES OF INTEREST

Tourist Information Centre (Summer only) - The Guildhall, Fore Street, East Looe. Tel: 01503 262072

◆ OLD GUILDHALL MUSEUM - Displays on local history housed in 15th century listed guildhall. Building retains many original features including the old magistrate's benches, cells and stocks. Exhibits include fishing, boat building, smuggling, lifeboat logs, minerals & porcelain. Higher Market Street, East Looe.

SPORT & LEISURE

◆ Parks & Gardens - Hannafore Road, West Looe. West Looe Downs, West Road, West Looe.

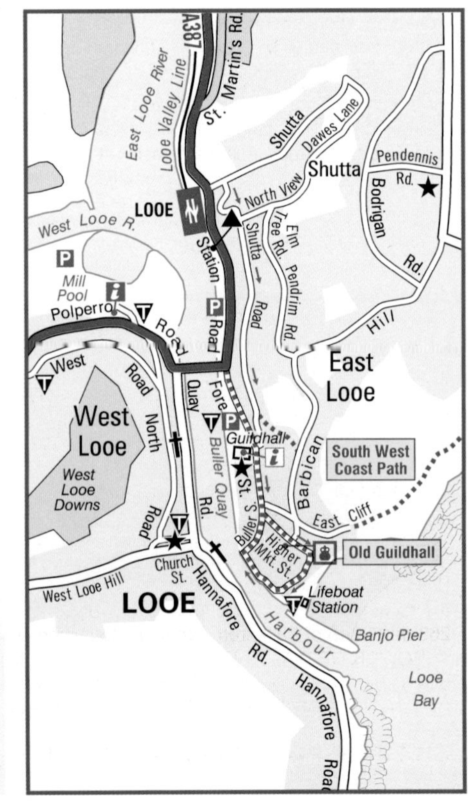

LYNTON and LYNMOUTH

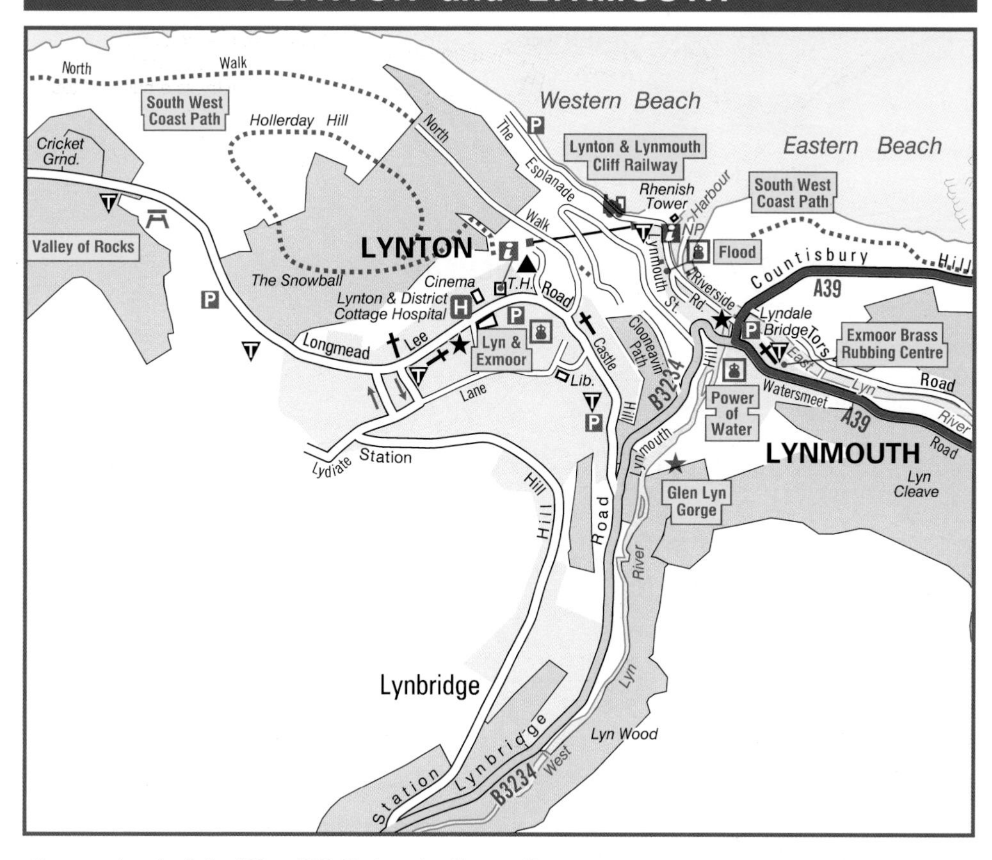

Separated vertically by 152 m (500 ft), the twin villages of Lynton and Lynmouth are linked by a unique water powered cliff railway. The vulnerability of Lynmouth's location lying on the shore where the valleys of the East and West Lyn converge made it the victim of the 1952 flood when 90 million gallons of water fell in a single night. The Rhenish Tower which was originally built in 1855 by Colonel Rawdon was rebuilt following its destruction in the disaster. Lynmouth was once famous for its large catches of herring and curing houses known as 'Red Herring Houses' lined both sides of the river. Lynton and Lynmouth developed rapidly as a tourist destination with its natural beauty and tranquility making it a favourable destination for the traveller. Today numerous walks exemplify the natural beauty of the area; paths over Hollerday Hill lead to the Valley of Rocks and Mars Hill is renowned for its thatched cottages.

PLACES OF INTEREST

Tourist Information Centre (All year) - Town Hall, Lee Road, Lynton. Tel: 01598 752225

◆ EXMOOR BRASS RUBBING CENTRE - Houses over 100 brass facsimiles dating from 1277. The collection which includes knights, clergy & animals is one of the largest available to the public. Woodside Craft Centre, Watersmeet Road, Lynmouth. ◆ GLEN LYN GORGE - Walks lead up through the woodland passing cascades & waterfalls to the ravine. Flood level marks from the 1952 catastrophe can be seen & England's largest privately owned hydro-electric station opened here in 1985. Watersmeet Road, Lynmouth. ◆ LYN & EXMOOR MUSEUM - Housed in a 17th century cottage the museum offers a comprehensive reflection of life in the area from the stone age to the modern day. St Vincent Cottage, Market Street, Lynton. ◆ LYNMOUTH FLOOD EXHIBITION - Exhibition recalls the devastation caused by the flood of 1952. Memorial Hall, Riverside Road, Lynmouth. ◆ LYNMOUTH VISITOR CENTRE (NP) - Displays recall the famous rescue of 1899 when the Lynmouth lifeboat was hauled 13 miles over land to launch at Porlock Weir. The Esplanade, Lynmouth. ◆ LYNTON & LYNMOUTH CLIFF RAILWAY - Officially opened in 1890, the railway is the last working water powered Victorian cliff railway in Europe. Rises 152 m (500 ft) over the 263 m (862 ft) of track from Lynmouth to Lynton. The Esplanade, Lynmouth & Lee Road, Lynton. ◆ POWER OF WATER EXHIBITION - Displays illustrate the various uses of water. Exhibition of steam engine models. Old Chapel, Glen Lyn Gorge, Watersmeet Road, Lynmouth. ◆ VALLEY OF ROCKS, THE - Famous dry valley thought to be a glacial meltwater channel formed during the Ice Age. Lynton.

ENTERTAINMENT ◆ Cinemas - Lee Road, Lynton.

MINEHEAD

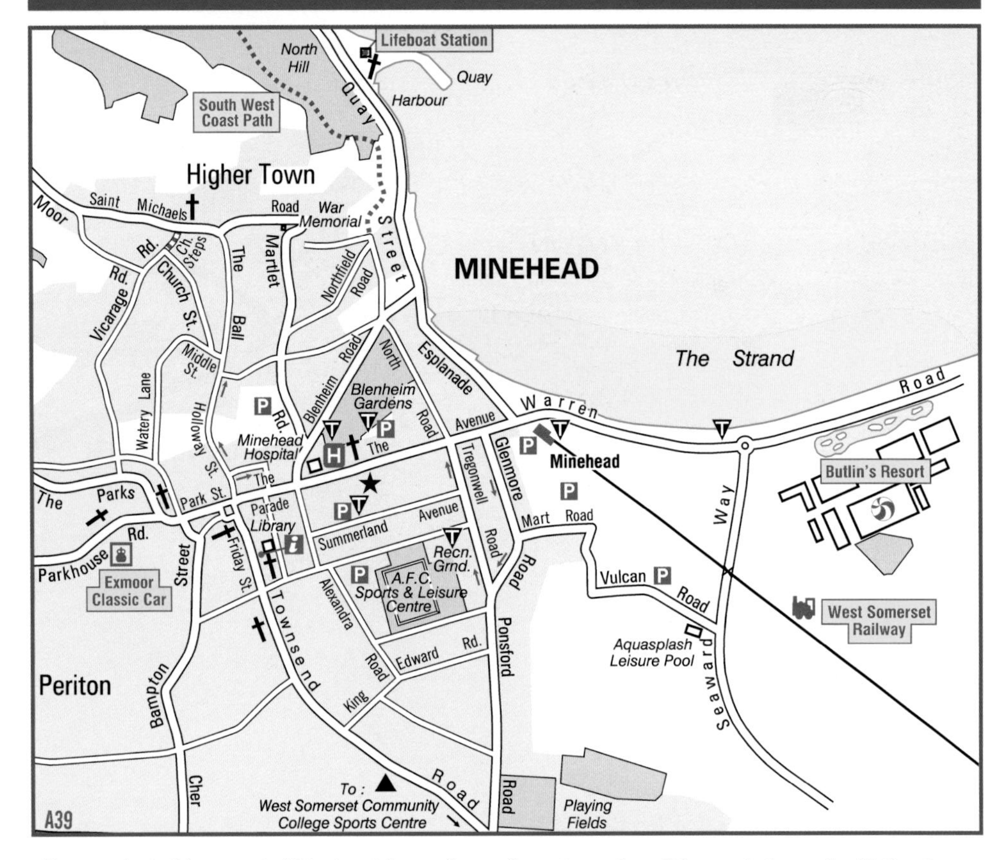

The popular holiday resort of Minehead lies on the north eastern edge of Exmoor between the National Park and the coast. The development of the town centred around the quay which offered safety and shelter on a coastal front that was both exposed and hazardous. The Higher Town retains much of its charm with thatched cottages and narrow alleyways, a favourite is Church Steps which leads up to the 14th century St Michael's Church on North Hill with spectacular views over the town. The old almhouses are on Market House Lane and nearby are the picturesque Blenheim Gardens. Minehead is the starting point of Britain's longest footpath, the 500 mile South West Coast Path.

PLACES OF INTEREST

Tourist Information Centre (All year) - 17 Friday Street. Tel: 01643 702624

◆ BUTLIN'S FAMILY ENTERTAINMENT RESORT - Large entertainment complex offering a diverse range of activities including sub-tropical waterworld with flume rides & rapids, funfair, leisure dome & boating lake. The Seafront, Warren Road. ◆ EXMOOR CLASSIC CAR COLLECTION - Collection of cars ranging from a 1923 Wolseley Colonial to a 1973 Ferrari Dino, motorbikes and rare automobilia. BT Telephone Exchange, Parkhouse Road. ◆ LIFEBOAT STATION - Established in 1901. Atlantic 75 class & Inflatable 'D' lifeboats. The Harbour. ◆ WEST SOMERSET RAILWAY - Steam trains run from Minehead to Bishop's Lydeard on the line that was closed by British Rail in 1971. The reopening of the line in 1976 created the longest independent railway in Britain. The Station, The Sea Front.

ENTERTAINMENT

◆ Cinemas - Butlin's Family Entertainment Resort (see above).
◆ Theatre - Regal Theatre, The Avenue.

SPORT & LEISURE

◆ Parks & Gardens - Blenheim Gardens, Blenheim Road.
◆ Sports Centres - West Somerset Community College Sports Centre, Bircham Road (SE Minehead).
◆ Swimming Pools - Aquasplash Leisure Pool, Seaward Way. Butlin's Somerwest World Holiday Centre (see above).
◆ Ten Pin Bowling - Butlin's Family Entertainment Resort (see above).

NEWQUAY

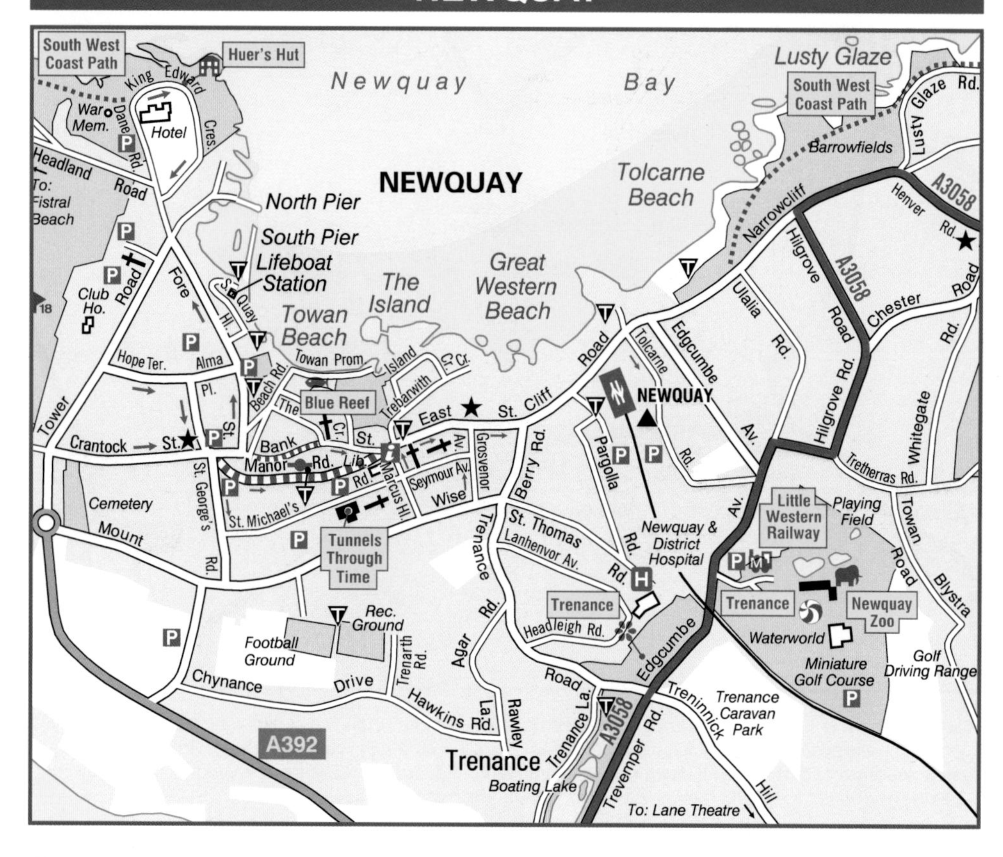

Newquay, Cornwall's favourite holiday resort, is famous for its Atlantic rollers, making it a centre for surfing, and for its expanses of sandy beaches of which west facing Fistral Beach (to the west of the town) is the largest and most popular. Once important as a fishing port, due largely to huge shoals of pilchards, and for the export of china clay, the town became a tourist destination with the coming of the railway in 1875.

PLACES OF INTEREST

Tourist Information Centre (All year) - Municipal Offices, Marcus Hill. Tel: 01637 871345

◆ HUER'S HUT - Small clifftop building from which lookouts, known as "Huers", watched for pilchard shoals. King Edward Crescent.

◆ BLUE REEF AQUARIUM - 70 species. Vast tropical ocean display with underwater walkthrough tunnel. Sharks, stingrays, seahorses. Lair of the Octopus. Underwater tunnel. Towan Promenade.

◆ NEWQUAY ZOO - 10 acres of lakeside gardens with over 300 animals including lions, monkeys, penguins, lemurs, sloths and reptiles. Tropical & Nocturnal Houses, Animal encounters, Dragon Maze, Tarzan Trail, Children's Farmyard. Trenance Leisure Park, Edgcumbe Avenue.

◆ TRENANCE GARDENS - Outstanding municipal gardens, boating lake. Trenance Road.

◆ TRENANCE LEISURE PARK - 26 acre sport & leisure park incorporating Waterworld, Newquay Zoo & Miniature Railway. Edgcumbe Avenue.

◆ TUNNELS THROUGH TIME - Recreation of the stories & legends of Cornwall using life-size figures and authentic costumes. Visit the Dungeon of Despair, witness the suffering of plague victims and discover the hazards of mining. St Michaels Road.

ENTERTAINMENT

◆ Theatres - Lane Theatre, Lane (SE of Newquay).

SPORT & LEISURE

◆ Parks & Gardens - Trenance Gardens (see above). Trenance Leisure Park (see above).

◆ Sports Centres - Newquay Sports Centre, Tretherras Road (E Newquay).

◆ Swimming Pools - Newquay Water World, Trenance Leisure Park.

NEWTON ABBOT

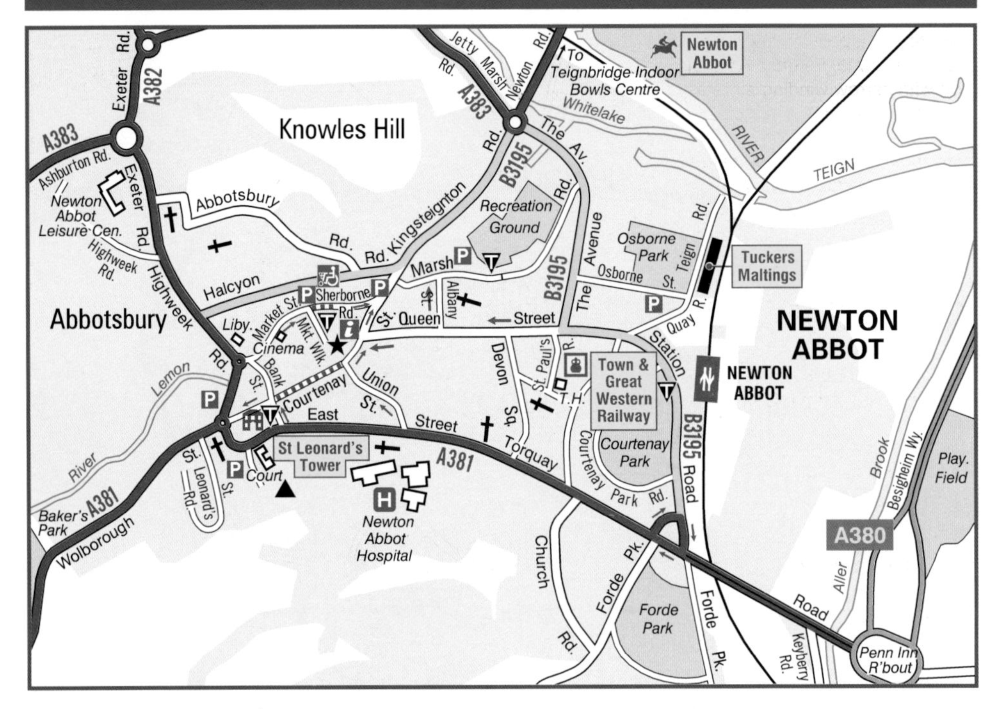

Newton Abbot is a busy market town and, since the arrival of the South Devon Railway in the mid 19th century, a railway town with typical railway terraces. It is situated at the head of the River Teign estuary where the Stover Canal brought down clay, and granite from quarries on Dartmoor served by the Haytor Granite Tramway, for export. The Templer Way follows much of the route.

PLACES OF INTEREST

Tourist Information Centre (All year) - 6 Bridge House, Courtenay Street. Tel: 01626 367494

◆ NEWTON ABBOT RACECOURSE - Between Newton Abbot & Kingsteignton. Newton Road.

◆ NEWTON ABBOT TOWN & GREAT WESTERN RAILWAY MUSEUM - History of town & its railway. Working signal box. GWR artifacts & photographs. 2a St Paul's Road.

◆ ST LEONARD'S TOWER - 14th century clock-tower (the remains of St Leonard's Church) where William III, Prince of Orange, was declared king in 1688. Courtenay Street.

◆ TUCKERS MALTINGS - Guided tours of traditional working malthouse where barley is turned into malt using original Victorian machinery. Teign Road, Osborne Park.

ENTERTAINMENT

◆ Cinemas - Market Street.

SPORT & LEISURE

◆ Parks & Gardens - Baker's Park, Wolborough Street. Courtenay Park, Courtenay Park Road. Forde Park, Forde Park. Osborne Park, Osborne Street.

◆ Sports Centres - Newton Abbot Leisure Centre, Wain Lane.

◆ Swimming Pools - Newton Abbot Leisure Centre (as above).

Fore Street, Totnes

PADSTOW

Padstow is a popular resort on the River Camel Estuary. A fishing port with narrow winding streets converging on the picturesque and ancient harbour, the town was once the western outpost of the London & South Western Railway, closed in 1967 and now the Camel Trail. The pagan 'Obby 'Oss festival is held on May Day to celebrate the coming of Summer. There are no beaches in Padstow however a ferry leaves from the North Quay, or Lower Beach at low tide, to beaches at Rock across the estuary.

PLACES OF INTEREST

Tourist Information Centre (All year) - Red Brick Building, North Quay. Tel: 01841 533449

◆ CAMEL TRAIL - Popular 17 mile cycleway & footpath on former railway line starting at Padstow and linking to Wadebridge & Bodmin.

◆ NATIONAL LOBSTER HATCHERY - Visitor centre detailing conservation work and local fishing industry. Witness development of the lobsters from egg to juvenility. South Quay.

◆ PADSTOW MUSEUM - Local history. Displays on Padstow lifeboat, customs, railway. Ship paintings. Town Library, The Institute, Market Place.

◆ PRIDEAUX PLACE - Elizabethan mansion completed in 1592. Formal garden & landscaped deer park. Tregirls Lane.

ENTERTAINMENT

◆ Cinemas- Lanadwell Street.

Padstow Harbour

PAIGNTON

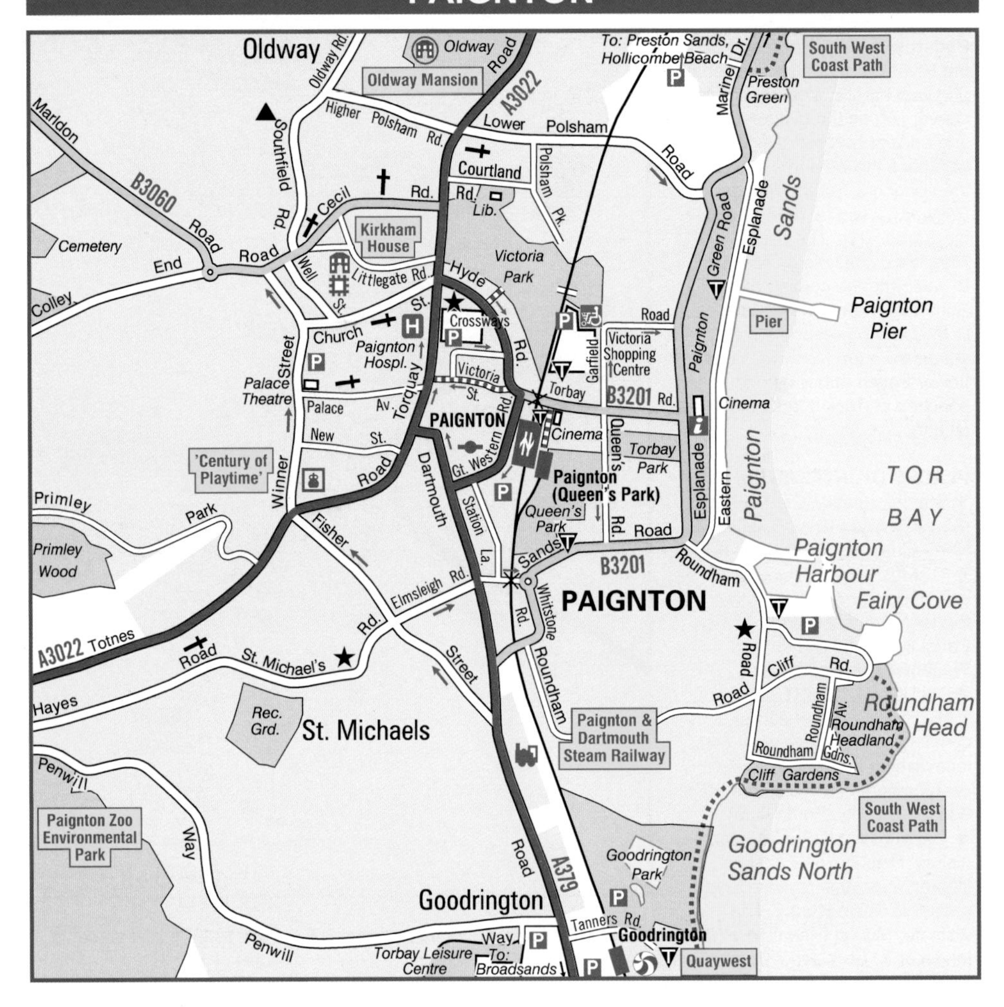

Paignton is a very popular family seaside resort which developed as a close neighbour of Torquay after the arrival of the railway in the mid 19th century. There are gardens, a pier, a long seafront (with the sandy beach of Paignton Sands adjacent to Paignton Green) and a small harbour at the end of the Esplanade. Other popular sandy beaches are Goodrington Sands, Broadsands to the south, and Preston Sands and Hollicombe Beach.

PLACES OF INTEREST

Tourist Information Centre (All year) - multiplex cinema, The Esplanade. Tel: 0870 707 0010

◆ 'CENTURY OF PLAYTIME'- DOLL & TOY MUSEUM - Old dolls & toys. 30 Winner Street.

◆ KIRKHAM HOUSE (EH) - 15th century stone merchant's town house. Old hall, furniture displays. Kirkham Street. ◆ OLDWAY MANSION - Begun by Isaac Singer (founder of the famous sewing machine company) in 1875 in the style of the Palace of Versailles with 17 acres of landscaped gardens. Torquay Road.

◆ PAIGNTON & DARTMOUTH STEAM RAILWAY - 7 mile standard gauge steam railway running along the scenic Torbay coast & Dart estuary to Kingswear. Stations also at Goodrington & Churston. Paignton (Queen's Park) Station, Torbay Road. ◆ PAIGNTON PIER - Amusements, childrens rides. Paignton Sands.

◆ PAIGNTON ZOO ENVIROMENTAL PARK - 75 acres of gardens with lions, tigers, elephant & giraffe house, ape centre, baboon rock, aviary.- Totnes Road. ◆ QUAYWEST - Waterpark with 8 water flumes including the highest in England at 20 m (65 ft). Swimming pools, amusement rides. Goodrington Sands.

ENTERTAINMENT

◆ Cinemas - Esplanade Road. Torbay Road. Theatres- Palace Theatre, Palace Avenue.

SPORT & LEISURE

◆ Parks & Gardens - Goodrington Park, Tanners Rd. Oldway, Torquay Rd.Paignton Green, Eastern Esplanade. Preston Green, Marine Drive. Queen's Park, Queen's Road. Roundham Headland & Cliff Gardens, Roundham Gardens. Torbay Park, Esplanade Road. Victoria Park, Hyde Road. ◆ Sports Centres - Torbay Leisure Centre, Clennon Valley, Penwill Way. ◆ Swimming Pools - Quaywest (see above). Torbay Leisure Centre (as above).

PENZANCE

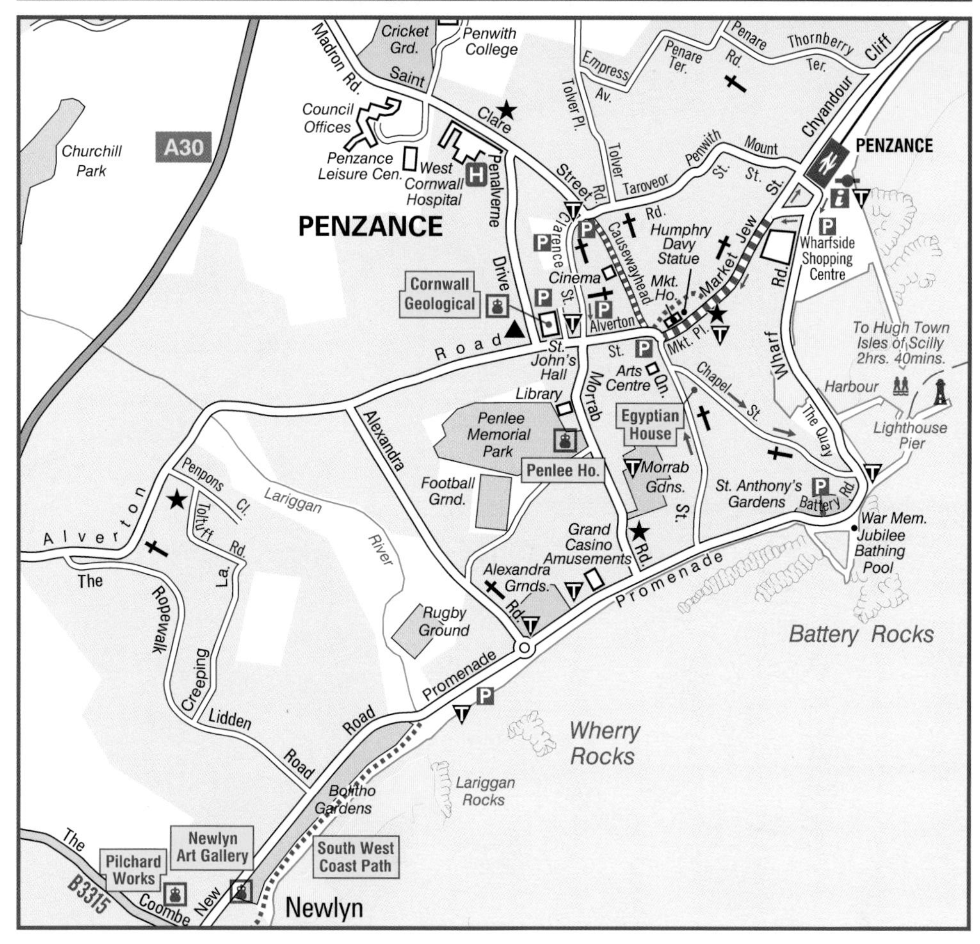

Penzance, a port and resort characterized by its 19th century granite buildings, has developed as a market town for West Cornwall, its status being promoted by becoming the western terminus of the former Great Western Railway. Buildings of note include the imposing domed Market House (1838) at the top of Market Jew Street with the statue of Sir Humphry Davy (born 1778), inventor of the miner's safety lamp, below it and St John's Hall on Alverton Street, built in the 1860s, one of the largest granite buildings in Britain. There are two parks with sub-tropical plants off Morrab Road. Regular ferries leave Lighthouse Pier for St Mary's in the Isles of Scilly; helicopter flights leave from the heliport off the A30 to the east of the town.

PLACES OF INTEREST

Tourist Information Centre (All year) - Station Road. Tel: 01736 362207

◆ EGYPTIAN HOUSE - Building with elaborate painted Egyptian style facade built in 1836. Owned by The Landmark Trust and used for holiday lettings. Chapel Street. ◆ NEWLYN ART GALLERY- Changing exhibitions of contemporary paintings & sculpture in Passmore Edwards building. Newlyn Green, New Road, Newlyn.

◆ PENLEE HOUSE GALLERY & MUSEUM - History of West Cornwall from stone age to present day. Largest art collection in West Cornwall dating from 1750 including artists of the famous Newlyn School. Morrab Road.

◆ PILCHARD WORKS - Britain's last working salt pilchard factory. Visitors can witness the salting and pressing process in action, talk to the staff and make their own stencil impressions. Photographs, paintings & artefacts are also on display. Tolcarne, The Coombe, Newlyn.

ENTERTAINMENT

◆ Cinemas - Causewayhead. Theatres - West Cornwall Arts Centre, Parade Street.

SPORT & LEISURE

◆ Parks & Gardens - Alexandra Grounds, Promenade. Bolitho Gardens, New Road, Newlyn. Morrab Gardens, Morrab Road. Penlee Memorial Park, Morrab Road. St Anthony's Gardens, Battery Road.

◆ Sports Centres - Penzance Leisure Centre, St. Clare St.

◆ Swimming Pools - Jubilee Bathing Pool, Battery Road.

◆ Ten-Pin Bowling - Grand Casino Amusements, Promenade.

PLYMOUTH

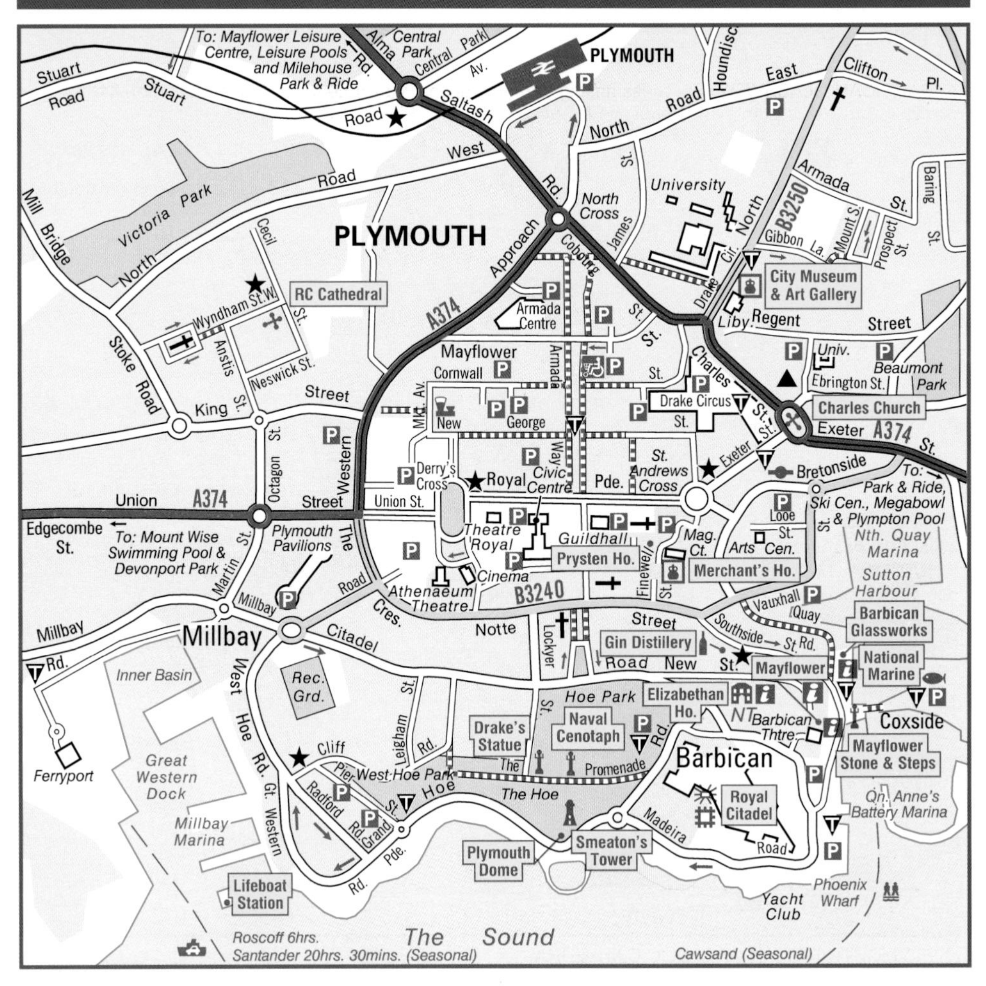

Plymouth is the largest city in the West Country. Associated with sailors such as Hawkins, Raleigh, Frobisher and Sir Francis Drake, the harbour of Plymouth Sound (protected by Rennie's one mile long breakwater of 1812-41), is a safe anchorage leading to the 300 acre Royal Navy Dockyard of Devonport founded in 1691. Pleasure cruises to view the warships depart from the Mayflower Steps and Phoenix Wharf. Much of the city centre (now rebuilt) was destroyed during a bombing raid in 1941, however, the Barbican area, part of the old quarter of Plymouth with narrow streets, survives.

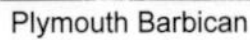
Plymouth Barbican

Drakes Island, Plymouth

PLACES OF INTEREST

Tourist Information Centre (All year) - Island House, The Barbican. Tel: 01752 306330

◆ BARBICAN GLASSWORKS - Glassmaking demonstrations. Visitor centre with information on the maritime & trading history of the Barbican & Sutton Harbour. Old Fishmarket, The Barbican.

◆ CITY MUSEUM & ART GALLERY - Collections of West Country art & porcelain including works by Sir Joshua Reynolds. Natural history. Drake Circus.

◆ CHARLES CHURCH - Bombed building & spire of 17th century church, left as a memorial to Plymouth's war dead. Charles Cross.

◆ DRAKE'S STATUE - Statue of 1884 of Sir Francis Drake overlooking The Hoe, where according to legend he was playing bowls when the Spanish Armada was first sighted in 1588. The Promenade, The Hoe.

◆ ELIZABETHAN HOUSE (NT) - Tudor sea captain's timber framed house. Period furnishings. National Trust Information centre. 32 New Street.

◆ MAYFLOWER STONE & STEPS - Memorial stone & steps where the Pilgrim Fathers sailed to America in 1620. The Barbican.

◆ MAYFLOWER VISITOR CENTRE - Story of the Pilgrim Fathers. The Barbican.

◆ MERCHANT'S HOUSE MUSEUM - 16th century Elizabethan building housing displays on the story of Plymouth including the Eddystone lighthouses, Plymouth's defences & the blitz. Victorian pharmacy. 33 St Andrews Street.

◆ NATIONAL MARINE AQUARIUM - UK's biggest aquarium with deepest tank in the UK. Deep Reef tank, Coral Seas tanks, Shark Theatre, World of Seahorses, Mediterranean tank, The Abyss. Plymouth Sound sealife, seashore life & rare preserved Giant Squid. Rope Walk, Coxside.

◆ NAVAL CENOTAPH - Tall monument commemorating those who died in both world wars. The Promenade, The Hoe.

◆ PLYMOUTH DOME - Life size replica Elizabethan Street. Displays include Plymouth seafarers, blitz devastation & ocean liners. Observation galleries over Plymouth Sound. The Hoe.

◆ PLYMOUTH GIN DISTILLERY - Guided Tours of 200 year old distillery on site of former friary. Audio-visual. Black Friars Distillery, 60 Southside Street.

◆ PLYMOUTH ROMAN CATHOLIC CATHEDRAL - Gothic Revival building of 1858 with 61 m (200 ft) spire. Cecil Street.

◆ PRYSTEN HOUSE - Stone built merchant's town house of 1498. By appointment only. Finewell Street.

◆ ROYAL CITADEL (EH) - Guided tours of England's largest 17th century fortress including Baroque main gate & royal chapel. The Hoe.

◆ SMEATON'S TOWER - Upper part of third Eddystone lighthouse built by John Smeaton in 1759, removed to The Hoe in 1882 when the sea undermined the rock on which it stood. The Hoe.

Smeaton's Tower, The Hoe Plymouth

ENTERTAINMENT

◆ Cinemas - Derry's Cross (two). Plymouth Arts Centre, Looe Street. ◆ Concerts - Plymouth Pavilions, Millbay Road. ◆ Theatres - Athenaeum Theatre, Derry's Cross. Barbican Theatre, Castle St. Theatre Royal, Royal Parade.

SPORT & LEISURE

◆ Ice Rink - Swiss Lake Ice Rink, Plymouth Pavilions, Millbay Road. ◆ Parks & Gardens - Beaumont Park, Tothill Avenue. Central Park, Alma Road. Devonport Park, Exmouth Road, Devonport (W Plymouth Freedom Fields, Lipson Road (E Plymouth). Hoe Park, West Hoe Park & The Hoe. Victoria Park, North Road West.

◆ Ski Slope - Plymouth Ski Centre, Longbridge Road (NE Plymouth). ◆ Sports Centres - Mayflower Leisure Centre, Central Park, Mayflower Drive. ◆ Swimming Pools - Atlantis Pool, Plymouth Pavilions, Millbay Road. Central Park Leisure Pools, Central Park, Mayflower Drive. Mount Wise Swimming Pool, Richmond Walk, Mount Wise (W Plymouth). Plympton Pool, Harewood Park, Plympton (NE of Plymouth). Seaton Pool, Brest Road, Crownhill (N Plymouth). ◆ Ten-Pin Bowling - Plymouth Superbowl, Plymouth Road, Plympton (NE of Plymouth).

ST. IVES

St. Ives, formerly one of the most important pilchard fisheries in Cornwall, is now a very popular holiday resort of great charm characterized by the old fishing quarter with its narrow steep cobbled streets, alleys and steps lined with stone cottages. Its setting and clarity of light led to its colonization by artists, notably Ben Nicholson and Barbara Hepworth in 1939. Beyond the harbour, with Smeaton's Pier, is The Island, a headland separating sheltered Porthgwidden Beach from Porthmeor Beach popular for surfing.

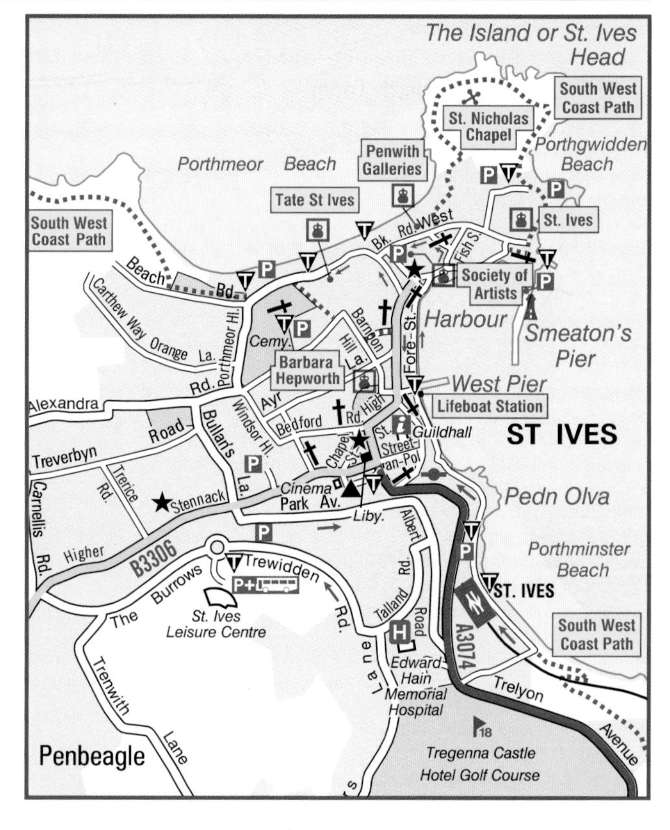

PLACES OF INTEREST

Tourist Information Centre (All year) - The Guildhall, Street-an-Pol.
Tel: 01736 796297

◆ BARBARA HEPWORTH MUSEUM & SCULPTURE GARDEN- The artist's former workshop displaying over 40 of her sculptures. Trewyn Studios, Barnoon Hill.
◆ PENWITH GALLERIES- Exhibitions of paintings & sculpture by the Penwith Society of Arts. Back Road West. ◆ ST IVES MUSEUM- Cornish & local history. Displays on fishing, lifeboat, maritime history, railways. Wheal Dream. St. Ives Society of Artists- Paintings & sculptures. Old Mariner's Church, Norway Square. ◆ ST NICHOLAS CHAPEL- Fishermans chapel which exhibited a guiding light prior to the lighthouses on Smeaton's Pier. The Island. ◆ TATE ST IVES - Outpost of London's Tate Gallery. Changing displays of 20th century modern art associated with St. Ives & Cornwall. Porthmeor Beach.

ENTERTAINMENT

◆ Cinemas - Royal Square.

SPORT & LEISURE

◆ Parks & Gardens - Trewyn Gardens, Back Street.
◆ Sports Centres - St. Ives Leisure Centre, Trenwith Burrows.

St. Ives

TAUNTON

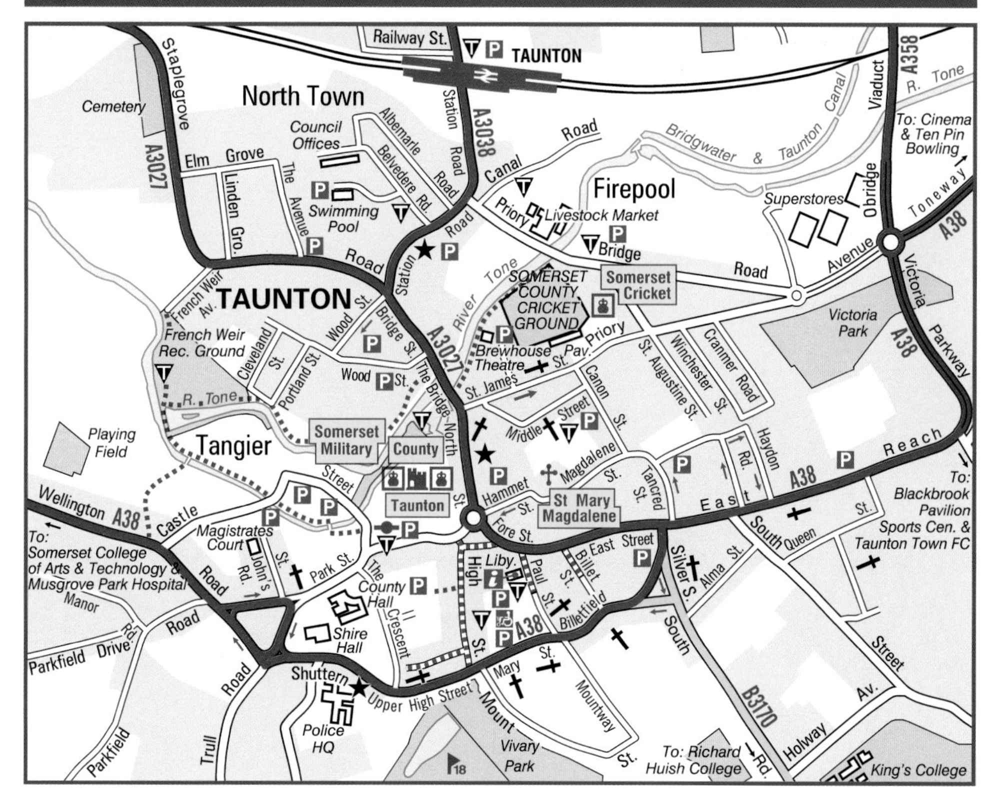

Founded in the 7th century by King Ina to guard the river crossing against the Celts, Taunton, 'the town on the Tone' is the county town of Somerset and home of the county's cricket ground. History has left its mark on the town and the heritage trail highlights many of the towns architectural features using distinctive brass plaques set in the pavement. Buildings of interest include the 14th century Tudor House in Fore Street, the oldest house in Taunton and Gray's Almshouses founded in 1635 by Robert Gray. Taunton developed in the 13th century as an important market and trading town. Today with a population of 60,000, it is still a lively centre with a diverse range of shopping facilities and a livestock market.

PLACES OF INTEREST

Tourist Information Centre (All year) - The Library, Paul Street. Tel: 01823 336344

◆ ST MARY MAGDALENE CHURCH - One of the largest & richest perpendicular churches in England. The 49.7m (163ft) tower dating from 1500 was rebuilt in the 19th century & local legend tells of how donkeys were used in the construction to haul the ropes of the pulley system to raise materials to the top. Upon completion of the tower, the donkeys were themselves raised to the top so they could see the view. Magdalene Street. ◆ SOMERSET COUNTY MUSEUM - A wide variety of exhibits are combined to reflect the history of Somerset. The collection includes dolls, toys, silver, pottery, fossils & archaeological items. Taunton Castle, Castle Green. ◆ SOMERSET CRICKET MUSEUM - Housed in a renovated priory barn, this extensive collection of cricket memorabilia reflects the history of the County Club from 1875. Adjacent to the County Cricket Ground. Priory Barn, 7 Priory Avenue. ◆ SOMERSET MILITARY MUSEUM, THE - Exhibition devoted to the history of the Somerset Light Infantry. Somerset County Museum, Taunton Castle, Castle Green. ◆ TAUNTON CASTLE - The remains of the 12th century castle now form part of the County Museum in the town centre. The Great Hall which survives today with some modifications was the scene of Judge Jeffries notorious Bloody Assize held after the collapse of Monmouth's Rebellion in 1685. Castle Green.

ENTERTAINMENT

◆ Cinemas- Heron Gate (E Taunton). Theatres- Brewhouse Theatre & Arts Centre, Coal Orchard.

SPORT & LEISURE

◆ Parks & Gardens - French Weir Park, French Weir Avenue. Goodland Gardens, Castle Street. Victoria Park, Victoria Parkway. Vivary Park, Mount Street.

◆ Sports Centre - Blackbrook Pavilion Sports Centre, Blackbrook Way (SE Taunton).

◆ Swimming Pools - Taunton Pool, Station Road.

◆ Ten Pin Bowling - Hollywood Bowling, Heron Gate (E Taunton).

TORQUAY

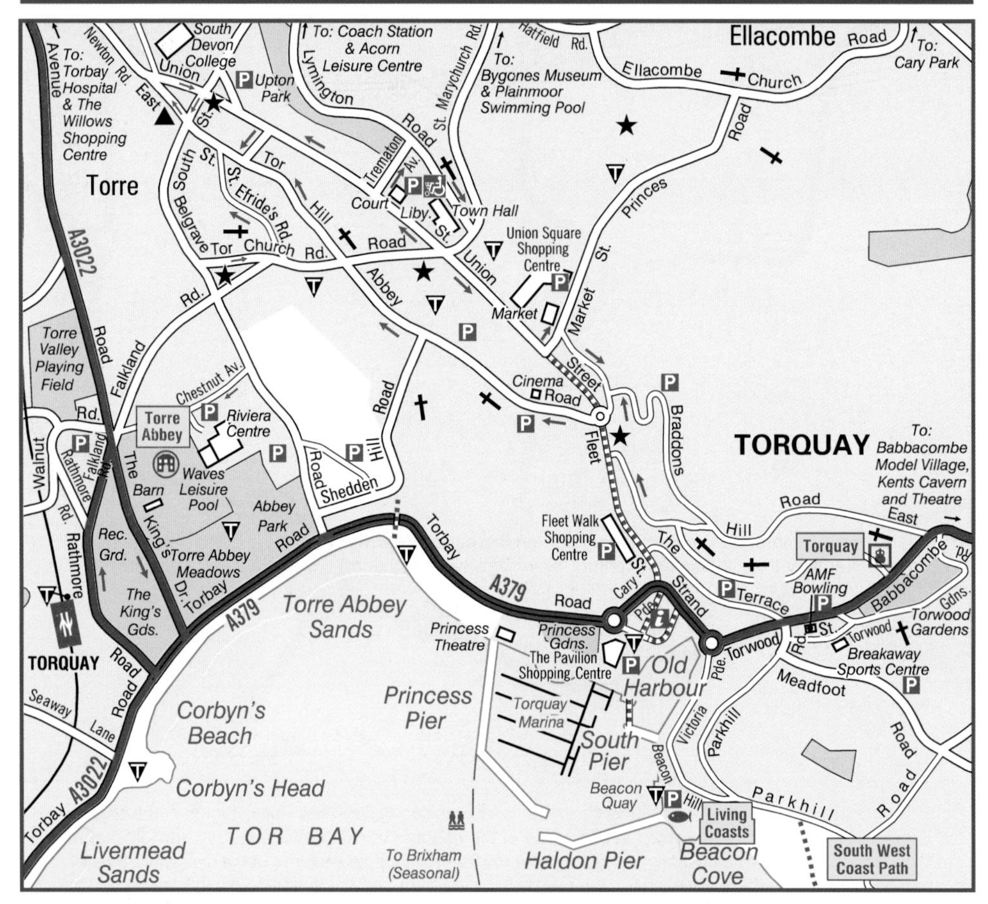

Tor Bay with the three main towns of Torquay, Paignton and Brixham is known as the 'English Riviera' due to the mild climate which supports gardens planted with sub-tropical plants including many palms, similar to those originally imported from New Zealand and the Mediterranean in the early 19th century. The planned streets of the town were first developed by the Cary family of Torre Abbey, the characteristic terraces being built in the first half of the 19th century. The harbour and Torquay Marina provide the focus for the town with the main shopping street of Union Street accessible via Fleet Walk. Torre Abbey Sands, one of over 20 beaches on the Riviera, provides a nearby sandy beach.

PLACES OF INTEREST

Tourist Information Centre (All year)- Vaughan Parade. Tel: 0870 707 0010

◆ LIVING COASTS - Largest aquarium in the West. Exotic tropical marine fish & local marine life. Reptiles & birds. Torquay Harbourside, Beacon Quay. ◆ TORQUAY MUSEUM - Local history, regimental, archaeology & natural history galleries. Victoriana. Agatha Christie exhibition. 529 Babbacombe Road.
◆ TORRE ABBEY - House closed until 2008. 18th century house with furnished period rooms, art galleries, chapel, formal gardens on remains of Premonstratensian abbey (founded in 1196) of which the gatehouse, guest hall & tithe (or Spanish) barn survive. The King's Drive.

ENTERTAINMENT

◆ Cinemas - Abbey Road. Theatres - Babbacombe Theatre, Babbacombe Downs, Babbacombe (NE of Torquay). Princess Theatre, Torbay Road.

SPORT & LEISURE

◆ Parks & Gardens - Abbey Park (& Torre Abbey Meadows), Torbay Road. Cary Park, Cary Avenue, Babbacombe (NE of Torquay). Princess Gardens, Torbay Road. Torwood Gardens, Torwood Gardens Road. Upton Park, Lymington Road. Victoria Park, Sherwell Lane (W Torquay). ◆ Sports Centres - Acorn Leisure Centre, Lichfield Avenue (N Torquay). Breakaway Sports Centre, Torwood Gardens Road. Riviera Centre, Chestnut Avenue. ◆ Swimming Pools - Riviera Centre (as above). Plainmoor Swimming Pool (Swim Torquay), Plainmoor (N of Torquay). ◆ Ten-Pin Bowling - AMF Bowling, Torwood Street.

TRURO

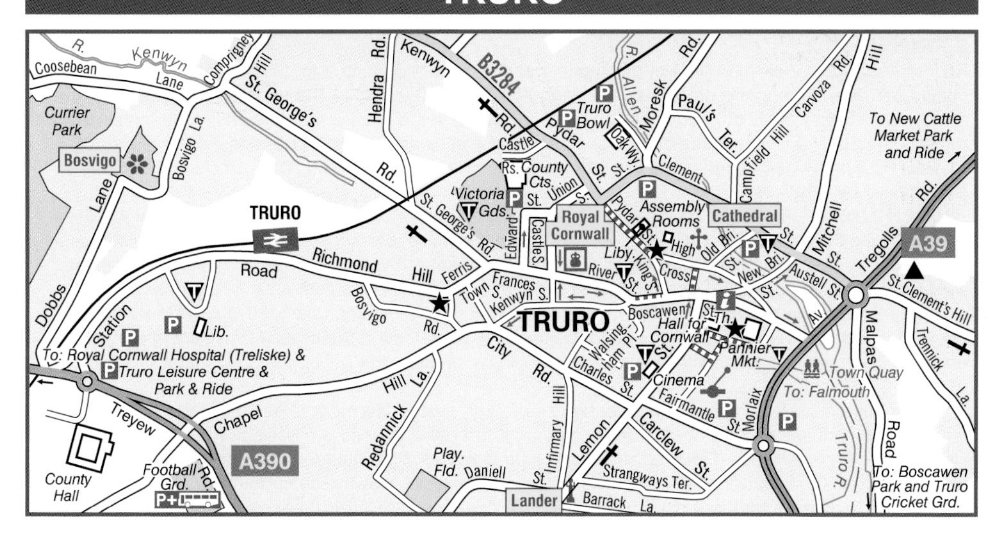

Truro grew up as a tin and copper exporting port on the navigable Truro River, and prospered from becoming a stannary town in the 18th century. Now Cornwall's cathedral city and administrative centre, the city is famous for its Georgian architecture exemplified by Boscawen Street, Strangways Terrace, Walsingham Place and Lemon Street (the finest Georgian Street in Cornwall). Buildings of note are the former Assembly Rooms of 1772 on High Cross and the granite City Hall built in the Italian style. Boat trips to Falmouth operate from Town Quay (or Malpas when the tide is low).

PLACES OF INTEREST

Tourist Information Centre (All year) - Municipal Buildings, City Hall, Boscawen Street. Tel: 01872 274555

◆ BOSVIGO GARDEN - 3 acres of enclosed & walled gardens with herbaceous & rare plants. Bosvigo Lane.

◆ LANDER MONUMENT - Tall granite column with statue of Richard Lander, killed exploring the River Niger in West Africa. Lemon Street.

◆ ROYAL CORNWALL MUSEUM - Displays include archaeology, local history, mining industry, seafaring, natural history, costumes, fine art. River Street.

◆ TRURO CATHEDRAL - Built between 1880 & 1910 in the Early English style; the first Anglican cathedral to be built in England since the rebuilding of St Paul's and the only cathedral in Cornwall. High Cross.

ENTERTAINMENT

◆ Cinemas - Lemon Street.

◆ Theatres - City Hall, Boscawen Street.

SPORT & LEISURE

◆ Parks & Gardens -
Boscawen Park, Malpas Road (SE of Truro).
Victoria Gardens, Castle Rise.

◆ Sports Centres -
Truro Leisure Centre, College Road (W of Truro).

◆ Swimming Pools -
Truro Leisure Centre (as above).

◆ Ten-Pin Bowling -
Truro Bowl, Oak Way.

Torbay Harbour

MOORS

BODMIN MOOR

Bodmin Moor, designated an area of outstanding natural beauty, is a remote, bleak heather covered upland granite moorland still grazed by moorland ponies and bisected by the main A30 road. Similar, but smaller and lower than Dartmoor, it was densely populated in the bronze age and has many archaeological remains. The best known are the three stone circles of The Hurlers, Rillaton Barrow and the hill fort of Stowe's Pound all near Minions, and the Stripple Stones Henge and Trippet Stone Circle on Hawkstor Downs near Blisland.

Natural features include Brown Willy, at 420 m (1,377 ft), the highest point on both Bodmin Moor and in Cornwall, and the rockier Roughtor, the second highest point, readily accesible from Camelford with over seventy hut circles on its north west slope. The Cheesewring, at Stowe's Hill near Minions, is a popular wind eroded granite formation of circular stones balanced on top of each other whilst the natural lake of Dozmary Pool, in the centre of the moor south of Bolventor, is according to legend where Sir Bedivere threw King Arthur's Sword Excalibur. Also at Bolventor is Jamaica Inn featured in the novel of the same name by Daphne du Maurier with Smugglers at Jamaica Inn tableaux & Daphne du Maurier memorial room.

Ruins of tin and copper mines can be seen to the south east of the moor at Minions and include the ruined engine houses of the Phoenix United and South Phoenix Mines. The Minions Heritage Centre is in Houseman's Engine House. Other attractions include Golitha Falls, managed by English Nature at the southern edge of the moor near Redgate and Wesley Cottage at Trewint, near Altarnun, where John Wesley, the founder of Methodism, stayed. There are reservoirs at Colliford Lake and Siblyback Lake Water Park.

Bodmin Moor

DARTMOOR

Dartmoor, one of the last great wildernesses of southern England, is a 365 square mile bleak granite upland with an average elevation of 366 m (1200 ft), designated a National Park in 1951. It is characterized by its coarse granite outcrops, or tors, and by large areas of isolated blanket peat bog covered with purple gorse and heather which provide rough grazing for the semi-wild Dartmoor ponies. The rapidly changing weather conditions, frequently with low cloud, heavy rain and fog, provided the setting for Conan Doyle's novel 'The Hound of the Baskervilles'. The heart of the moorland is crossed by only two significant roads meeting at Two Bridges, near Princetown with its infamous prison of 1806 the only town of any size. Remains of mining can be found at the Vitifer Tin Mine and the Wheal Betsy Pumping Engine House at Mary Tavy. Granite quarrying developed in the 19th century, the largest quarries were at Haytor and Foggintor (where stone for Nelson's Column in London was quarried).

The moor was extensively farmed in the bronze age when the climate was milder, and is covered in prehistoric remains such as the Merrivale Prehistoric Settlement, Grimspound near Postbridge and the remote Stall Moor and Butterdon stone rows. The moor has many medieval stone clapper bridges examples being at Postbridge, Bellever and Dartmeet.

The Ministry of Defence training area in the north part of the moor (with live firing- observe warning signs), has the two highest points of High Willhays (621 m, 2038 ft) and Yes Tor (619 m, 2030 ft). Other tors to the west of the moor are Great Staple Tor, Great Mis Tor and Vixen Tor, with a sphynx like profile, the tallest rock pile on Dartmoor at 27 m (90 ft) from base to top, near Merrivale. Hound Tor, with its deserted medieval village, the popular Haytor Rocks, with its granite tramway and Blackingstone Rock, 24 m (80 ft) above ground level with Victorian iron steps, are in the east.

There are many beauty spots in the river valleys around the edge of the moor. In the east is Fingle Bridge (near the famous Castle Drogo), Lustleigh Cleave, Becky Falls and Canonteign Falls near Hennock comprising Lady Exmouth Falls, at 67 m (220 ft) England's highest waterfall. In the west is Lydford Gorge and the more open Tavy Cleave. To the south is the Dewerstone Rock; the 50 m (165 ft) high crags form the finest rock climbing face in inland Devon. The granite 'chimney' Bowerman's Nose is near Manaton and the intriguing Ten Commandments Stone is at Buckland in the Moor.

MOORS

EXMOOR (see also Lynton and Lynmouth description)

Exmoor is mainly defined by the 267 square miles of the Exmoor National Park created in 1954. Comprising a plateau of sedimentary rocks and slate regularly reaching 400 m (1312 ft), it does not have the rugged granite tors of Bodmin Moor and Dartmoor, but is more remote and less crowded. The western edge rises sharply whilst the Brendon Hills to the east have the gentlest contours. The 30 square mile Exmoor Forest at Simonsbath (never in fact forested), were once a royal deer park. The area typifies the bleak upland moorland with coarse grass, bracken, heather and gorse especially seen at The Chains, a waterlogged wilderness forming the head waters of the Exe, Barle and West Lyn rivers.

Deep thickly wooded valleys make up the lower sections of the moor, many of which are accessible only by walking. Heddon's Cleave (200 m, 656 ft deep), is reached by footpath from Hunter's Inn, Badgworthy Water from Malmsmead, and Horner Wood (at 900 acre, one of the largest ancient oak woodlands in the country), by trails through the valley of Horner Water. Accessible by car is the National Trust owned Watersmeet, a popular beauty spot at the junction of the steep wooded valleys of the East Lyn River and Hoaroak Water east of Lynmouth.

There is spectacular scenery on the coast with a series of headlands interrupted only by the Vale of Porlock. Notable are the cliffs at Countisbury, at around 137 m (450 ft) the highest in Devon, and the striking Little Hangman near Combe Martin.

Exmoor is well known for large numbers of red deer and the native Exmoor ponies. Oare Church and Robber's Bridge are famous for their associations with R.D. Blackmore's novel 'Lorna Doone'. Doone Valley (actually Hoccombe Combe) is reached either by a 2 mile walk from Malmsmead along the valley of Badgworthy Water (which runs along the Devon Somerset border), or across Brendon Common.

Tarr Steps over the River Barle (at 55 m or 180 ft long with 17 spans), is the finest example of a clapper bridge in the country (best approached from the B3223 at Winsford Hill), Landacre Bridge is a preserved medieval bridge in a moorland setting near Withypool Common, whilst the scenic Bury Packhorse Bridge is near Dulverton. Exmoor's tallest standing stone, the 3 m (9 ft) high Longstone, and Chapman Barrows bronze age burial mounds, are near Challacombe. Dunkery Beacon at 519 m (1704 ft) is the highest point on Exmoor and in Somerset, whilst Western Common, near Kinsford Gate, at 493 m (1617 ft) is the highest point on Exmoor within Devon. From here, a desolate road follows the ridge along the Somerset border south east for 9 miles to West Anstey Common where the 13 ton Hancock Memorial Stone was erected in 1935 in memory of a local hunter. Other notable places are Culbone Church, near Porlock with its scenic toll roads, thought to be the smallest complete parish church in England and the town of Dunster, famous for its castle and gardens and early 17th century octagonal Yarn Market.

Portchapel Beach, Cornwall

ISLES OF SCILLY

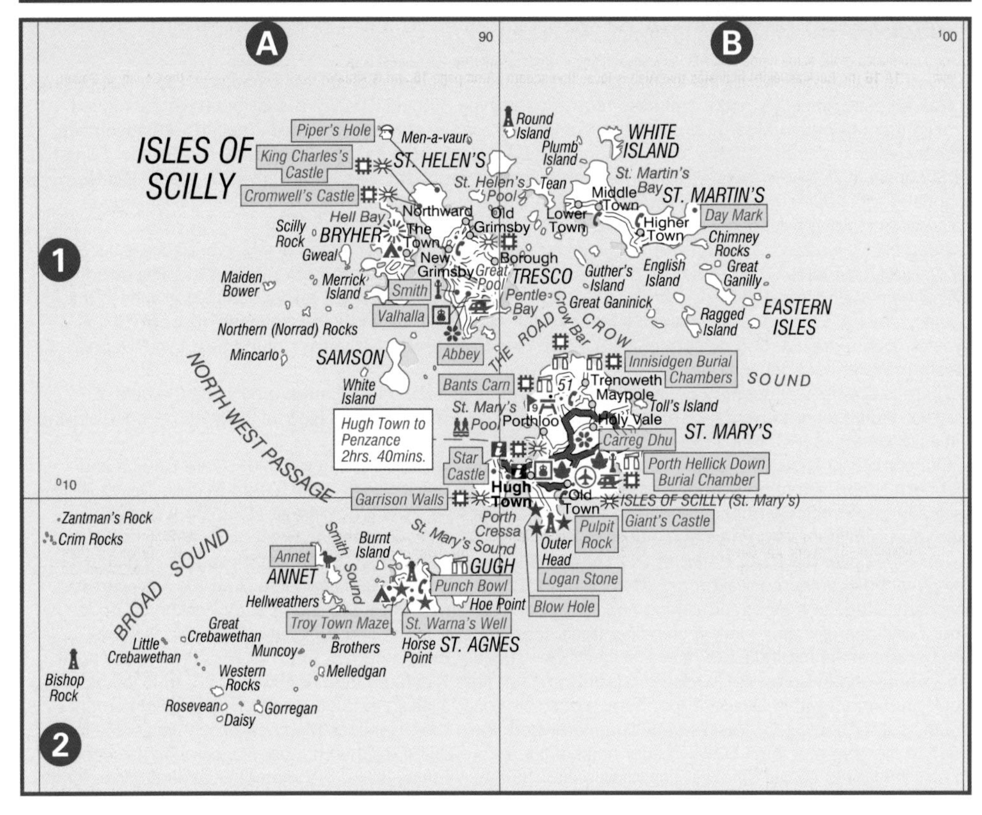

Tourist Information Centre (All year) - The Old Wesleyan Chapel, Garrison Lane, Hugh Town, St Mary's. Tel: 01720 422536

The Isles of Scilly, an archipelago of about 150 granite islands, islets and rocks, 28 miles south west of Land's End, are according to legend, the only visible relic of Lyonesse, the land of Arthurian legend. The islands have many bronze age cairns and iron age remains. With a very mild climate, the chief industry outside tourism is floriculture, with spring flowers grown in tiny sheltered fields being exported as early as November. The five largest islands are populated- St Mary's, Tresco, Bryher, St Martin's and St Agnes. Seals and seabirds abound on the many uninhabited islands and the autumn migration of both sea and land birds is renowned. Hugh Town, St Mary's where launches leave to all the off islands, is reached by ferry and helicopter from Penzance and plane from Land's End Aerodrome (St Just).

St Mary's is the largest island with most of the population centred on the capital Hugh Town, situated on the isthmus to The Garrison peninsula fortified by a 1.5 mile long granite wall punctuated with batteries, and Star Castle (now a hotel). The Isles of Scilly Museum is in Church Street and the Isles of Scilly Wildlife Trust Visitor Centre is on the Quay. To the north of the island are the bronze age Bant's Carn Burial Chamber and iron age Halangy Down Ancient Village; the best preserved bronze age burial mound being at Porth Hellick Down to the south. On the south coast Old Town Bay churchyard has the graves of 120 people lost in the wreck of the German trans-atlantic liner 'Schiller' in 1875 and Porth Hellick has a monument to Rear-Admiral Sir Cloudesley Shovell lost with the Association and three other ships in 1707 on the Western Rocks. Peninnis Head has the overhanging Pulpit Rock, Logan Stone weighing over 300 tons, and many naturally eroded granite shapes. Telegraph Hill is the highest point on St Mary's and Scilly at 51 m (167 ft).

Tresco is famous for its Tresco Abbey sub-tropical Gardens, on the site of a 12th century benedictine priory (of which an archway survives), and the Valhalla Collection of 19th century ships figureheads from vessels lost around the islands. The contrasting rugged north end of the island beyond New Grimsby has King Charles's Castle, the 17th century Cromwell's Castle, the Old Blockhouse harbour gun tower at Old Grimsby and Piper's Hole, a natural cave with pool.

Bryher is noted for the rocky coast at Shipman Head and Hell Bay on the wild northern part of the island.

St Martin's is known for its fine beaches on the south side. A large pepper pot navigation mark- the Day Mark of 1685, is on Chapel Down on the east tip. St Agnes has the Troy Town Maze on the Downs, set in pebbles by an 18th century keeper of St Agnes Lighthouse (built 1680 and disused in 1911), the second oldest surviving purpose built lighthouse in the country. Also of note is the the Punch Bowl, a curiously perched boulder on Wingletang Down. 4 miles south west, past the bird sanctuary on Annet, is Bishop Rock Lighthouse (built in 1851-8 and rebuilt in 1883-7) one of Britain's tallest lighthouses guarding the treacherous waters around the Western Rocks, the scene of many shipwrecks.

INDEX TO CITIES, TOWNS, VILLAGES, HAMLETS & LOCATIONS

(1) A strict alphabetical order is used e.g. Ashprington follows Ash Moor but precedes Ash Priors.

(2) The map reference given refers to the actual map square in which the town spot or built-up area is located and not to the place name.

(3) Where two or more places of the same name occur in the same County or Unitary Authority, the nearest large town is also given;
e.g. Aish. *Devn* . . . .1A **16** (nr. Buckfastleigh) indicates that Aish is located in square 1A on page **16** and is situated near Buckfastleigh in the County of Devon.

(4) Major towns are shown in bold; i.e. **Bideford.** *Devn* 1C **27**

(5) Towns which have a second page reference appear on a Town Plan; i.e. Bude. *Corn* . . . . 3A **26** & **42**

COUNTIES AND UNITARY AUTHORITIES with the abbreviations used in this index

Cornwall : *Corn*
Devon : *Devn*
Dorset : *Dors*
Isles of Scilly : *IOS*
North Somerset : *N Som*
Plymouth : *Plym*
Somerset : *Som*

A

B

L

M

N

T

Selected Places of Interest and Other Features

HOW TO USE THE PLACES OF INTEREST INDEX

Places of interest are represented by the appropriate symbol on the map together with red text in a yellow box. The index reference is to the square in which the symbol (or its pointer) appears, not to the text box; e.g. Hartland Abbey —1A **26** is to be found in square 1A on page **26**. The page number being shown in bold type.

Entries shown without a main map index reference have the name of the appropriate town plan on which they appear. For reasons of clarity, these places of interest do not appear on the main map pages. The extent of these town plans are indicated on the main map pages by a blue box.

Terms such as 'museum', 'country park' etc. are omitted from the text on the map.

Entries in italics are not named on the map but are shown with a symbol.
Entries in italics and enclosed in brackets are not shown on the map.
For both these types of entry, the nearest village or town name is given, where that name is not already included in the name of the place of interest.

Places of interest that are open for the summer season only are shown with an S symbol after the index reference.

Opening times for places of interest vary considerably depending on the season, day of week or the ownership of the property. Please check with the nearest tourist information centre listed below before starting your journey.

EH, English Heritage Site. NT, National Trust Property - Always open. NT, National Trust Property - Restricted opening. NP, National Park Property - Always open

Tourist Information Centre (Open All Year)

*Ashburton Information Centre — 1B **16**, Tel: 01364 653426*
*Axminster — 1C **25**, Tel: 01297 34386*
*(Barnstaple — 3D **33**, Tel: 01271 375000)*
*Bideford — 1C **27**, Tel: 01237 477676 / 421853*
*Bodmin — 1C **13**, Tel: 01208 76616*
*Braunton — 3C **33**, Tel: 01271 816400*
*Bridgwater — 3C **37**, Tel: 01278 427652*
*(Brixham — 2D **17**, Tel: 0870 707 0010)*
*Bude — 3A **26**, Tel: 01288 354240*
*Budleigh Salterton — 2A **24**, Tel: 01395 445275*
*Burnham-on-Sea — 2D **37**, Tel: 01278 787852*
*Chard — 3D **31**, Tel: 01460 65710*
*Combe Martin — 2D **33**, Tel: 01271 883319*
*Crediton — 3C **29**, Tel: 01363 772006*
*(Dartmouth — 2C **17**, Tel: 01803 834224)*
*Dawlish — 3D **23**, Tel: 01626 215665*
*(Exeter — 1D **23**, Tel: 01392 265700)*
*Exmouth — 2D **23**, Tel: 01395 222299*
*(Falmouth — 1C **9**, Tel: 01326 312300)*
*(Fowey — 2D **13**, Tel: 01726 833616)*
*Great Torrington — 2C **27**, Tel: 01805 626140*
*Helston & Lizard Peninsula — 3D **7**, Tel: 01326 565431*
*Holsworthy Visitor Information Centre — 3B **26**, Tel: 01409 254185*
*Honiton — 3B **30**, Tel: 01404 43716*
*Ilfracombe — 2D **33**, Tel: 01271 863001*
*Isles of Scilly, St Mary's — 1B **66**, Tel: 01720 422536*
*Ivybridge — 2A **16**, Tel: 01752 897035*
*Kingsbridge — 3B **16**, Tel: 01548 853195*
*Launceston — 2B **20**, Tel: 01566 772321*
*Liskeard — 1A **14**, Tel: 01579 349148*
*Looe, East Looe — 2A **14**, S, Tel: 01503 262072*
*Lostwithiel — 2D **13**, Tel: 01208 872207*
*Lyme Regis — 1D **25**, Tel: 01297 442100*
*Lynton — 2B **34**, Tel: 01598 752225*
*Mevagissey — 3C **13**, Tel: 0870 443 2928*
*Minehead — 2D **35**, Tel: 01643 702624*
*(Newquay — 1A **12**, Tel: 01637 854020)*
*Newton Abbot — 3C **23**, Tel: 01626 215667*
*Ottery St Mary — 1A **24**, S, Tel: 01404 813964*
*(Padstow — 3B **18**, Tel: 01841 533449)*
*(Paignton — 1C **17**, Tel: 0870 707 0010)*
*(Penzance — 2B **6**, Tel: 01736 362207)*
*Perranporth — 2D **11**, Tel: 01872 573368*
*Plymouth (Discovery Centre), Crabtree, Plymouth — 2D **15**, Tel: 01752 266030 / 266031*
*(Plymouth (Mayflower) — 2C **15**, Tel: 01752 306330)*
*St Austell — 2C **13**, Tel: 0870 445 0244*
*(St Ives — 1C **7**, Tel: 01736 796297)*
*Salcombe — 3B **16**, Tel: 01548 843927*
*Seaton — 1C **25**, Tel: 01297 21660*
*Sidmouth — 2B **24**, Tel: 01395 516441*
*Somerset Visitor Centre, M5 (Southbound), East Brent — 1D **37**, Tel: 01934 750833*
*Taunton — 1C **31**, Tel: 01823 336344*
*Tavistock — 3C **21**, Tel: 01822 612938*
*Teignmouth — 3D **23**, Tel: 01626 215666*
*Tiverton — 2D **29**, Tel: 01884 255827*
*(Torquay — 1D **17**, Tel: 0906 680 1268)*
*Totnes — 1C **17**, Tel: 01803 863168*
*(Truro — 3A **12**, Tel: 01872 274555)*
*Wadebridge — 3B **18**, Tel: 0870 122 3337*
*Wellington — 1B **30**, Tel: 01823 663379*
*Weston-super-Mare — 1D **37**, Tel: 01934 888800*
*Whiddon Down — 1A **22**, Tel: 01647 231375*
*Woolacombe — 2C **33**, Tel: 01271 870553*

Tourist Information Centre (Summer Season Only)

*Bovey Tracey — 3C **23**, S, Tel: 01626 832047*
*Camelford — 2D **19**, S, Tel: 01840 212954*
*Crewkerne — 2D **31**, Tel: 01460 73441*
*Hayle — 2C **7**, Tel: 01736 754399*
*Langport — 1D **31**, Tel: 01458 253527*
*Modbury — 2A **16**, S, Tel: 01548 830159*
*Okehampton — 1D **21**, S, Tel: 01837 53020*
*Shaldon Tourism Centre — 3D **23**, S, Tel: 01626 873723*
*South Molton — 1B **28**, S, Tel: 01769 574122*
*Watchet Tourism Office — 2A **36**, S, Tel: 01984 634565*

Visitor Centre/Information Centre (National Park)

Combe Martin Visitor Centre — 2D **33**, *Tel: 01271 883319*
County Gate Visitor Centre, Countisbury — 2B **34**, Tel: 01598 741321
*Dulverton Visitor Centre — 1D **29**, Tel: 01398 323841*
*Dunster Visitor Centre — 2D **35**, Tel: 01643 821835*
*Exmoor National Park Visitor Centre, Lynmouth — 2B **34**, Tel: 01598 752509*
*Haytor Information Centre, Haytor Vale — 3B **22**, Tel: 01364 661520*
High Moorland Visitor Centre, Princetown — 3D **21**, Tel: 01822 890414
*Moretonhampstead Visitor Information Centre — 2B **22**, Tel: 01647 440043*
*Newbridge Information Centre, Poundsgate — 3B **22**, Tel: 01364 631303*
*Postbridge Information Centre — 3A **22**, Tel: 01822 880272*

Visitor Centre/Information Centre (National Trust)

Carnewas (Bedruthan Steps) Information Centre, Trenance NT — 1A **12**, Tel: 01637 860563
*Cornwall Industrial Discovery Centre, Pool NT — 1D **7**, Tel: 01209 315027*
Fyne Court Visitor Centre, Broomfield NT — 3C **37**, Tel: 01823 451587
Heddon Valley Shop Information Centre, Martinhoe NT — 2A **34**, Tel: 01598 763402
*(Plymouth Elizabethan House Information Centre NT — 2C **15**, Tel: 01752 253871)*
*Selworthy Information Centre NT — 2D **35**, Tel: 01643 862745*
*Sexton's Cottage Information Centre, Widecombe in the Moor NT — 3B **22**, Tel: 01364 621321*

Abbey/Priory

See also Cathedral, Church/Chapel

Buckfast Abbey — 1B **16**
Cleeve Abbey EH — 2A **36**
Dunkeswell Abbey (remains of) — 2B **30**
*(Exeter St Nicholas Priory (remains of) — 1D **23**)*
Frithelstock Priory (remains of) — 2C **27**
*Launceston St Thomas's Priory (remains of) — 2B **20***
Muchelney Abbey (remains of) EH— 1D **31**, S
Tavistock Abbey (remains of) — 3C **21**

Animal Collection

See also Farm Park, Wildlife Park, Zoo

Buckfast Butterfly Farm & The Dartmoor Otter Sanctuary — 1B **16**
Devonshire Traditional Breed Centre — 1C **23**
Donkey Sanctuary, The — 2B **24**
*(Donkey Stables, Clovelly — 1B **26**)*
Ferne Animal Sanctuary — 3C **31**
Heaven's Gate Farm (Somerset Animal Rescue Centre) — 3D **37**
Miniature Pony Centre, The — 2B **22**
Monkey Sanctuary, The — 2A **14**
Mousehole Wild Bird Hospital & Sanctuary — 3B **6**
National Seal Sanctuary — 2B **8**
Prickly Ball Farm (Hedgehog Hospital) — 1C **17**
Shaldon Wildlife Trust — 3D **23**
Tamar Otter & Wildlife Centre, The — 2A **20**
Tamar Valley Donkey Park, The — 3C **21**
Tortoise Garden — 3B **12**

Aquarium

*(Blue Reef Aquarium, Newquay — 1A **12**)*
*(Brixham Aquarium — 2D **17**)*
*(Fowey Marine Aquarium — 2D **13**, S)*
*Ilfracombe Aquarium — 2D **33***
*(Living Coasts, Torquay — 1D **17**)*
Lyme Regis Marine Aquarium (& Cobb History) — 1D **25**
Mevagissey Harbour Marine Aquarium — 3C **13**
*(National Marine Aquarium, Plymouth — 2C **15**)*
*SeaQuarium, Weston-Super-Mare — 1D **37***

rboretum/Botanical Garden

e also Garden

rt Gallery

viary/Bird Garden

attle Site

ridge

Castle

See also Castle & Garden, Fortress

Castle & Garden

See also Castle, Fortress

Cathedral

See also Abbey, Church/Chapel, Priory

Children's Play Centre

Church/Chapel/Holy Well

See also Abbey, Cathedral, Priory

Cidermaker/Distillery

See also Vineyard

Country Park

Farm Park/Open Farm

See also Animal Collection, Wildlife Park, Zoo

Forest Park/National Park

Forest Walk/Nature Trail

Fortress

Garden

Hill Fort

istoric Building

istoric Building & Garden

orse Racecourse

Industrial Monument

Leisure Park / Leisure Pool

Lighthouse

Long Distance Footpath

Mine/Cave

Monument/Folly

Museum

Natural Attraction

Nature Reserve/Bird Sanctuary (English Nature, RSPB, The Wildfowl & Wetlands Trust, selected only)

See also Forest Walk

Place of Interest (General)

Prehistoric Monument

See also Hill Fort

Railway (Heritage, Narrow Gauge, Miniature)

Roman Remains

Theme Park

Vineyard

See also Cidermaker

Visitor Centre/Information Centre

Wildlife Park

See also Animal Collection, Farm Park, Zoo

Windmill

See also Industrial Monument

Zoo/Safari Park

See also Animal Collection, Farm Park, Wildlife Pa…

Photo credits:

Barnabys Picture Library — Front Cover River Fowey; Back Cover St. Ives; P.1 St Michaels Mount; P.4 North Cornish Coast; P.39 (bottom right) Clovelly; P.41 Brixham; P.44 Exeter Cathedral, Tudor Buildings Exeter; P.45 Dart Valley; P.47 River Fowey; P.55 Padstow Harbour; P.58 Plymouth Barbican, Drake Island Plymouth; P.59 Smeaton's Tower, The Hoe Plymouth; P.60 St. Ives.

Corbis Images — P.39 (bottom left) Hartland Point, Bryan Pickering; P.40 Cornish Countryside, Andrew Brown; P.42 Coastline Cornwall, Sally A. Morgan; P.43 River Dart, Patrick Ward; P.49 Ilfracombe, Paul Thompson; P.54 Fore Street, Totnes, Ric Ergenbright; P. 63 Torbay Harbour, Bryan Pickering; P.64 Bodmin Moor, Andrew Brown; P.65 Portchapel Beach, Adam Woolfit.